The World Cup

The World Cup

by Walt Chyzowych

Icarus Press

South Bend, Indiana

1982, 1984

The World Cup
Copyright ©1982 by Walt Chyzowych

Icarus Press, Inc.
Post Office Box 1225
South Bend, Indiana 46624

84 85 10 9 8 7 6 5 4 3 2

Library of Congress Cataloging in Publication Data

Chyzowych, Walter
  The World Cup.

    1. World Cup (Soccer)—History.   2. Soccer—United
States.   I. Title.
GV943.49.C49   1982   796.334′66   82-9223
ISBN 0-89651-900-7   AACR2
ISBN 0-89651-905-8 pbk.

To the memory of Miro Rys,
a young player of brilliance
cut down tragically in his prime.
He is missed.

Contents

Introduction

SOCCER'S GROWTH IN AMERICA OVER THE PAST DECADE HAS FAR SURPASSED ALL other team sports both in player participation and spectator attendance at all levels of competition. The projection for the 1980s: the soccer boom will double.

Soccer is the only sport in the world that can boast total international involvement. Consider that there are now 146 member nations of the Federation Internationale de Football Association (FIFA) involved in international play. Soccer has the largest membership of any sport in the world. Moreover, devotion to the sport by its fans and players is rabid. When major matches are played, crowds of over 100,000 at stadia and TV audiences in the millions are the rule, not the exception. As an international sport, even the Olympics pale in comparison with soccer's supreme tournament, the World Cup.

Every young American soccer player should set goals for himself to determine the level of play he can achieve. Even though at this time in American soccer history, very few American players are aware of the international aspects of the game, they should educate themselves about the international scene. One of the purposes of this book is to give all soccer-involved individuals a history of the World Cup, including U.S. participation since its inception in 1930.

As a player and coach, I was fortunate to be at both sides of the touchline for World Cup competition. Growing up in the Philadelphia area and raised with a soccer ball by the Philadelphia ethnic community (Ukrainians, Germans, and Irish), my dreams were to play for the U.S. World Cup team and to wear the red-and-blue U.S. shirt. Competing against foreign countries was the greatest honor one could hope for. Never would I have thought that after my playing career was over, I would have the privilege of coaching the U.S. World Cup team, as well as the Olympic and Youth World Cup teams.

Certainly my dreams were fulfilled, and I hope that every young American soccer player (over 2 million strong in organized play) will aspire to play for the U.S. and some day bring the Cup to America.

This book will provide, indirectly, some valuable information to all soccer people and, in turn, will help all active players to become more aware and prepared for this greatest of all tournaments, staged around the world every four years.

I
The History and Development of the World Cup

FIFA, THE GOVERNING BODY OF ALL SOCCER IN THE WORLD, IS THE ORGANIZATION responsible for staging the World Cup games. All directives and organizational aspects of the Youth World Cup and Senior World Cup come from the Zurich office in Switzerland, with the organizing committee making the final recommendations on where the World Cup should be held. The president of FIFA, currently Dr. Joao Havelange of Brazil, and his executive committee put the final stamp of approval on the site of this world-class competition.

The World Cup tournament was the brainstorm of Jules Rimet, president of FIFA from 1921 to 1954 and president of the French Football Association. The concept was proposed at the Antwerp (Belgium) Congress in 1920 and was formally adopted in 1928 during the FIFA Congress held in Amsterdam. To honor him for his role in bringing this idea to reality, the World Cup trophy was named the Jules Rimet Cup in 1946.

FIFA was founded in 1904 by seven original countries—Denmark, Belgium, France, Spain, Sweden, the Netherlands, and Switzerland. By the time the first World Cup tournament was staged in 1930, the membership had increased to twenty-six nations. In that first tournament, however, there were political problems and half of the countries withdrew to leave only thirteen countries competing in the host nation of Uruguay.

Five host countries have won the Cup (Uruguay, 1930; Italy, 1934; England, 1966; West Germany, 1974; and Argentina, 1978); two have lost the final and come in second (Brazil, 1950, and Sweden, 1958); one (Chile, 1962) came in third; and two others (Switzerland, 1954, and Mexico, 1970) have made it to the quarterfinals despite being dubious finalists at best. Only one country (Brazil, 1958, in Sweden) has ever won the World Cup played outside its own continent. Home-team advantage seems to be even stronger in soccer than, say, in football or basketball.

Originally, the format for the tournament was to include four pools with four countries in each. However, because of insufficient numbers participating in the first World Cup, there was only one pool of four and three pools of three each, designed to produce semifinalists who met in a straight knockout to determine the two finalists. The following years, 1934–38, a knockout system was used all the way through. These were the first years, however, that utilized a system of qualification resulting in a final round of sixteen teams.

World War II interrupted World Cup play, and it was not until 1950 that the tournament was revived. The format once again changed with the elimination of knockout semifinals and finals. The final pool now included the winner from each of the four groups with the World Cup champion being determined by a point system.

Other changes occurred in the format of the tournament, whereby in 1958, '62, and '66, two teams from each group emerged via a league system to a quarterfinal stage, from which point it became a sudden-death affair. In 1970 in Mexico, *goal difference* rather than *goal average* was used to separate team standings on points. And, in 1974, still another change occurred in West Germany, where two further qualifying groups replaced the quarter and semifinals, leaving two winners to playoff in the final and the two runners up playing for third and fourth places.

This system was applied again in Argentina in 1978. However, the 1982 format again has changed. Where in the past sixteen nations participated in the final World Cup competition, the new format, initiated by FIFA President Dr. Havelange, will have twenty-four nations competing for the FIFA World Cup trophy. The new formula combines both minileagues and knockout semifinals. The first stage will consist of six groups of four. In the second round, the top two teams from each group compete in four groups of three teams each. Two knockout semifinals are then played between the group winners, followed by the third-place match and the final.

The site selection for the tournament is determined on a rotating basis. The idea is to stage the tournament over as many of the six regions of the world as possible. These continental groupings are as follows; Africa; CONCACAF (North and Central America and the Caribbean): CONMEBOL (South America); UEFA (Europe); Asia; and Oceana.

The requirements to host the World Cup are that the country interested must have reasonable stadia with field dimensions of 75 yards by 120 yards, grass turf, and proper seating. In addition, the availability of air transportation as well as hotel accommodations are of major importance. Considering the fact that over 2 billion people viewed the 1982 The World Cup final from Spain, either by TV or by personal attendance, it is of utmost importance that these conditions are met in order to stage a successful World Cup.

The United States is in the CONCACAF region, which is considered an underdeveloped region as far as soccer is concerned. In the past, only the champions entered the World Cup final round. However, Dr. Havelange successfully convinced the FIFA membership that more countries from the underdeveloped soccer areas of the world should be included in the final round. As a result, both the champion and the runner-up from the CONCACAF region are now to be included among the final twenty-four nations.

The Youth World Cup

The Youth World Cup games had their beginning in 1977 when FIFA received sponsorship from Coca Cola International for the tournament to be played every two years. The age qualifications stipulate that players must be twenty or under when the finals are being held.

The first Youth World Cup games were played by sixteen qualifying nations in Tunisia in 1977. The success of this tournament encouraged Coca Cola to sponsor the 1979 Youth World Cup in Japan as well as the 1981 Youth World Cup in Australia.

II
The World Cup Finals

The First World Cup
Uruguay, 1930

site: Montevideo
13 entrants; FIFA membership 41

format: 4 groups, winners to go to
         semifinals

After Uruguay's impressive Olympic victories of 1924 (over Switzerland) and 1928 (over Argentina), Montevideo was chosen as the site for the first World Cup games. Uruguay's federation was willing to defray all expenses of participating countries, and the Uruguayans had built a magnificent new stadium in Montevideo. Even so, only four European countries—France, Belgium Romania, and Yugoslavia—traveled to the small South American

Argentina's Guillermo Stabile raises his hand in triumph after equalizing to make the score 1–1 during the World Cup final against Uruguay. Uruguay went on to win 4–2 to take the first Cup crown, but Stabile was the scoring champion of the series.

5

Above: The victorious Uruguayans pose after their triumph. Players from left to right: (kneeling) Alvaro Gestido, Jose Nazassi, Enrique Ballestrero, Ernesto Masqueroni, Jose Leandro Andrade; (standing) Lorenzo Fernandes, Pablo Dorado, Hector Scarone, Hector Castro, Pedro Cea, and Santos Iriarte.

Top: Uruguay's fourth and last goal in the final was scored by Hector Castro (just to the left of the right-hand post), known as "El Manco" (one-arm) because his right arm was cut off at the elbow.

country (France making its commitment only a month prior to the start of the games. Even in the Western Hemisphere, only two non-South American teams, the United States and Mexico, traveled to the games. The U.S. team was made up largely of foreign-born players, principally from England and Scotland.

Being on home turf, having strung out a couple of Olympic wins, and seeing most of the more powerful European teams fail to come to the games made the Uruguayans strong favorites. Moreover, they prepared for the contest with two months' splendid isolation in a luxury hotel in Prado Park in Montevideo. Hewing to a monastic regimen to the point of sending home their brilliant goalkeeper Mazzali when he had the temerity of breaking curfew, they fielded an impressive lineup of talent, led by a strong midfield line (Jose Andrade, Alvaro Gestido, and Lorenzo Fernandez).

Few other teams could boast of having had proper preparation for the tournament. Traveling by sea, it took three weeks to reach Uruguay from Europe. The men who made up these teams were not full-time professionals; many, in fact, had competed in the Olympics in 1924 and 1928. Ordinarily, such men held other jobs and trained only once or twice a week. Therefore, we can assume that the quality of play was not physically or technically optimal—part-time soccer players could only do so much.

With this first World Cup began the opportunity to identify great international players. Until then, little was known of these players outside their own country or area. One might read about them, but almost never did such players have the chance to prove themselves against the best from other countries. Prior to the World Cup, one might gainfully classify players as regards clubs, leagues, even nations, but with the advent of the World Cup, one could truly begin to speak of *world-class players*—not the best of this area or the best of the amateurs, but simply the best.

One such player was Luisito Monti, the brilliant center half of Argentina. His country built a formidable attack around him. Despite the fact that they had lost their great left wing, Raimondo Orsi, to Juventus of Italy after the 1928 Olympics, Argentina would likely provide the strongest challenge to Uruguay. This was underlined by the closeness of the Uruguay-Argentina battle for the 1928 Olympic gold (1–1 and 2–1). Sad to say for the Argentinians, Monti too would be lured away by Juventus after the games, and in 1934 he and his teammate Orsi would help *Italy* win the World Cup.

Here too began the noting of the contrasting styles of play among various regions of the world—the Europeans working harder and being less technical, and the Latins being more technical and less physical.

In Group 1 (Argentina, Chile, France, and Mexico), trouble seemed to be the byword. First there was the Argentina-France match in which the South American team held a slim 1–0 lead on the protested free-kick goal of Monti, when the referee blew for time over five minutes early. The French protested, the pitch was cleared, the game resumed, but the score remained the same. Argentina's next game was a wild melee, distinguished by the awarding of five penalty kicks. But the next match was the worst. Just before halftime a brawl broke out, requiring the aid of the local gendarmes to quell. (Argentina prevailed 3–1.)

Group 3 (Uruguay, Romania, and Peru) was by contrast rather relaxed, although not exceptionally well played for the home team. Peru had shown nothing much against Romania, losing 3–1 in the opener, but they were about as much as Uruguay could handle. After squeaking out a 1–0 win, Uruguay rested two forwards, Castro and Petrone, while its team beat Romania 4–0.

In Group 2 (Yugoslavia, Brazil, and Bolivia), the main interest settled around the surprise victory of Yugoslavia over Brazil, and Group 4 (the U.S., Paraguay, and Belgium) had its own special moment when the U.S. team overpowered Paraguay (which had beaten Uruguay in their last international before the World Cup) 3–0 after having turned away Belgium by an identical score. The stage was set for the semifinals: Argentina v. the United States and Yugoslavia v. Uruguay.

Argentina, leading by a goal by Monti at the half, overpowered the British-led American team with three more quick goals, and with that the spirit of the U.S. team broke, and the game ended with a 6–1 onslaught.

Uruguay too massacred game Yugoslavia, overcoming a momentary lead by the European team with a devastating attack (they were ahead 3–1 at the half, 6–1 at the final whistle). And so to the final—Uruguay v. Argentina.

Boatloads of Argentine fans poured across the Rio de la Plata to fill Centenary Stadium to cheer on their heroes—Stabile of Argentina and Cea of Uruguay—vying for the scoring title. Despite extraordinary safety precautions, the only real controversy seemed to settle on the ball—both teams wanted to use their own for the final. Like Solomon before him (though without the necessity of slicing the balls in half), the referee, Jean Langenus of Belgium, sagely solved the problem by playing half the game with one team's ball and half with the other's. Argentina won the toss and the right to use their ball first. Result: 2–1 Argentina at the half.

Ah, but Uruguay lost the toss and thereby gained the right to use their ball last. Result: 4–2 Uruguay. Which only goes to prove that the game isn't over until it's over.

The first Cup went to the deserving Uruguay team. It established the rather embarrassing trend toward home-team victors. But Uruguay would not compete again in World Cup play for twenty years. And when they came back, they would win it all again.

1930 (Uruguay)

GROUP 1

France (3)**4**	**Mexico** (0)**1**		
(Laurent, Langiller, Maschinot 2)	(Carreno)		
Argentina (0)**1**	**France** (0)**0**		
(Monti)			
Chile (1)**3**	**Mexico** (0)**0**		
(Vidal, Subiabre 2)			
Chile (0)**1**	**France** (0)**0**		
(Subiabre)			
Argentina (3)**6**	**Mexico** (0)**3**		
(Stabile 3, Varal-lo 2, Zumelzu)	(Lopez, Rosas F., Rosas M.)		
Argentina (2)**3**	**Chile** (1)**1**		
(Stabile 2, Evar-isto M.)	(Subiabre)		

	GP	W	D	L	GF	GA	Pts
Argentina	3	3	0	0	10	4	6
Chile	3	2	0	1	5	3	4
France	3	1	0	2	4	3	2
Mexico	3	0	0	3	4	13	0

GROUP 2

Yugoslavia (2)**2**	**Brazil** (0)**1**		
(Tirnanic, Beck)	(Neto)		
Yugoslavia (1)**4**	**Bolivia** (0)**0**		
(Beck 2, Mariano-vic, Vujadinovic)			

Brazil (1)**4**	**Bolivia** (0)**0**		
(Visintainer 2, Neto 2)			

	GP	W	D	L	GF	GA	Pts
Yugoslavia	2	2	0	0	6	1	4
Brazil	2	1	0	1	5	2	2
Bolivia	2	0	0	2	0	8	0

GROUP 3

Romania (1)**3**	**Peru** (0)**1**		
(Staucin 2, Barbu)	(Souza)		
Uruguay (0)**1**	**Peru** (0)**0**		
(Castro)			
Uruguay (4)**4**	**Romania** (0)**0**		
(Dorado, Scarone, Anselmo, Cea)			

	GP	W	D	L	GF	GA	Pts
Uruguay	2	2	0	0	5	0	4
Romania	2	1	0	1	3	5	2
Peru	2	0	0	2	1	4	0

GROUP 4

USA (2)**3**	**Belgium** (0)**0**		
(McGhee 2, Pate-naude)			
USA (2)**3**	**Paraguay** (0)**0**		
(Patenaude 2, Florie)			
Paraguay (1)**1**	**Belgium** (0)**0**		
(Pena)			

	GP	W	D	L	GF	GA	Pts
USA	2	2	0	0	6	0	4
Paraguay	2	1	0	1	1	3	2
Belgium	2	0	0	2	0	4	0

SEMIFINALS

Argentina (1)**6**	**USA** (0)**1**		
(Monti, Scopelli, Stabile 2, Peucelle 2)	(Brown)		
Uruguay (3)**6**	**Yugoslavia** (1)**1**		
(Cea 3, Anselmo 2, Iriarte)	(Seculic)		

FINAL (Montevideo, 7/30/30))

Uruguay (1)**4**	**Argentina** (2)**2**		
(Dorado, Cea, Iriarte, Castro)	(Peucelle, Stabile)		

Uruguay: Ballesteros; Nasazzi, Mascheroni; Andrade, Fernandez, Gestido; Dorado, Scarone, Castro, Cea, Iriarte

Argentina: Botosso; Della Toree, Paternoster; Evaristo, J., Monti, Suarez; Peucelle, Varallo, Stabile, Ferreira, Evaristo, M.

Referee: Langenus (Belgium)

The Second World Cup
Italy, 1934

site: Rome, Florence, Naples, Turin, Trieste

29 entrants: FIFA membership 46

format: Knock-out (single elimination)

The Italians under Mussolini had lobbied long and hard to become the host nation for the 1934 World Cup. FIFA held eight congresses before assenting to Italy's promise to run the games at a loss if necessary. The Fascist regime had something to prove, and they went about winning in a blatant way.

For the first time, FIFA conducted preliminary competitions to produce the sixteen finalists, and the finals were played on a knock-out (or single-elimination) basis. The lineup was much more impressive here, although Cup holders Uruguay decided not to attend (the only time that has ever happened)—and well they might. Their

The Italian soccer championship team, from left to right: (kneeling) Bertonili, Guiata, Meazza, Borel, de Maria, and Orsi; (standing) manager Pozzo, Combi, Mozeglio, Allemandi, Ferraris, and Monti.

1934 team was but a shadow of the 1930 winners. Besides, Uruguay had other concerns: a player strike, their fear of losing even more of their best players to European teams, and their resentment that Europe had not better supported the games in Montevideo.

Italy demolished a U.S. team much weaker than its 1930 counterpart 7-1, the sole American goal coming from Donelli, a Neapolitan who would be the only player from the finals to stay behind to play for Italy.

Other opening-round results— Germany defeated a relatively weak Belgium team 5-2; Brazil, one of the eight seeded teams by Italy, bowed to Spain 3-1; Czechoslovakia looked lackluster against Romania, winning 2-1; Hungary handed Egypt a 4-2 loss; Switzerland upset the Dutch 3-2; Sweden did the same to Argentina by an identical score; and, in the surprise of the first round, France gave the highly rated Austrian team a real run for it, losing 3-2 on a score by Schall, which he conceded years later to have been an offside goal.

Two quarterfinal matches were marred by violence and cowardly refereeing. Italy was to play the underrated Spanish team, whose brilliant captain-goalkeeper Ricardo Zamora had frustrated them in the past and seemed now to be taking on the entire Italian nation. Spain led at the half by a goal, but Italy's Ferrari equalized in the second half on a goal in which Schavio interfered with Zamora. But the referee did nothing, the goal stood, and the game ended in a draw. The violence of the game and the weak officiating led to numerous injuries. Seven Spaniards and four

Italians needed to be replaced for the replay of the game.

The next day's rematch was played in front of Mussolini; needless to say, the backbones of the officials did not stiffen overnight—three more injuries for Spain and two goals disallowed— and eventually a goal by Meazza led to a 1-0 win for Italy. The Swiss referee, Mercet, was later suspended by his own national association—small consolation to the ousted Spanish team.

The other violent quarterfinal match, between old rivals Austria and Hungary, was more a brawl than a soccer game. Austria took the lead 2-0 with goals from Horwath and Zischek. Sarosi scored one on a penalty kick but lost their right wing, Markos, to a red card, so the score stood 2-1.

Germany methodically and uninterestingly took care of Sweden 2-1 in a heavy rain in Milan, and Czechoslovakia overcame a game Swiss team 3-2 in what was surely the best of the quarterfinal games. Czechslovakia's Planicka's brilliance in the nets was almost overcome by the gallant Swiss team, which took the lead early in the game only to have it wiped out just before the half. Then Czechoslovakia led 2-1, and it was Switzerland's turn to equalize. Finally, the great Nejedly scored with seven minutes to go, and the game resulted in a 2-1 Czech win.

Germany's slow and plodding play was no match against the quick and subtle Czechs in the semifinal game at Rome. Result: 3-1 Czechoslovakia. Italy and Austria played their match in Milan's heavy rain, which hampered the close skills of the Austrians more than the Italians. Result: 1-0 Italy.

The final was memorable, as both

sides played brilliantly and scorelessly for seventy minutes. Then Czechoslovakia's Puc, who had been taken out with a leg cramp, came back to take a corner, had the ball returned to him, and shot the ball past Combi. Italy's fans became hysterical—some even had to be restrained from threatening members of the Czech team.

Then, with eight minutes to go, occurred one of those freak plays that immortalize World Cup play and become the subject of controversy for years and years. Orsi (remember him?) took a pass from Guaita, feinted to his left and shot instead to his right. But the ball somehow curled over the outstretched Planicka and dipped into the net (the next day, Orsi tried

unsuccessfully twenty times to repeat it with an empty net). The Italians had a new lease on life, and thirty minutes were added to the game. In the extra time, Italy's fit team shone—enough for Czechoslovakia to mark the limping Meazza a little more loosely than they normally would. This led to the Italian goal as Meazza found space and passed to Guaita, who served to Schiavio, who dribbled past one defender and blasted the ball into the goal.

Italy's 2–1 victory capped a controversial Cup, marred by violence, weak refereeing, and home-team advantage played to the hilt. Though sweet for Mussolini, outside Italy it soured in the mouth.

1934 (Italy)

FIRST RROUND

Italy (3)7 (Schiavio 3, Orsi 2 Meazza, Ferrari)	**USA** (0)1 (Donelli)
Czech. (0)2 (Puc, Nejedly)	**Romania** (1)1 (Dobai)
Germany (1)5 (Conen 3, Kobierski 2)	**Belgium** (2)2 (Voorhoof 2)
Austria (1)(1)3 (Sindelar, Schall, Bican)	**France** *(1)(1)2 Nicolas, Verriest*)
Spain (3)3 (Iraragorri*, Langara 2)	**Brazil** (1)1 (Silva)
Switzerland (2)3 (Kielholz 2, Abegglen)	**Netherlands** (1)2 (Smit, Vente)
Sweden (1)3 (Jonasson 2, Kroon)	**Argentina** (1)2 (Belis, Galateo)

*Penalty kick goal

Hungary (2)4 **Egypt** (1)2
(Teleky, Toldi 2, (Fawzi 2)
Vincze)

SECOND ROUND

Germany (1)2 (Hohmann 2)	**Sweden** (0)1 (Dunker)
Austria (1)2 (Horwath, Zischek)	**Hungary** (0)1 (Sarosi)
Italy (0)(1)1 (Ferrari)	**Spain** (1)(1)1 (Regueiro)
Italy (1)1 (Meazza)	**Spain** (0)0
Czech. (1)3 (Svoboda, Sobotka, Nejedly)	**Switzerland** (1)2 (Kieholz, Abegglen)

SEMIFINALS

Czech. (1)3 (Nejedly 2, Krcil)	**Germany** (0)1 (Noack)

Italy (1)1 **Austria** (0)0
(Guaita)

THIRD PLACE GAME (Naples)

Germany (3)3 **Austria** (1)2
(Lehner 2, Conen) (Horwath, Seszta)

FINAL (Rome, 6/10/34)

Italy (0)(1)2 **Czech.** (0)(1)1
(Orsi, Schiavio) (Puc)

Italy: Combi; Monzeglio, Allemandi; Ferraris, Monti, Bertolini; Guaita, Meazza, Schiavio, Ferrari, Orsi
Czechoslovakia: Planicka; Zenisek, Ctyroky; Kostalek, Cambal, Krcil; Junek, Svoboda, Sobotka, Nejedly, Puc

Referee: Eklind (Sweden)

The Third World Cup
France, 1938

sites: Paris, Toulousse, Rheims,
         Strasbourg, Le Havre, Antibes,
         Lille, Bordeaux, Marseilles
26 entrants; FIFA membership 51

format: Knock-out (single elimination)

Uruguay and Italy had shown how significant the home advantage was for soccer in winning the first two Cups on their own turf. In 1938, however, the home team, France, was not to win.

The Italian Cup holders returned with an even more impressive team, led by the veteran Meazza, one of only two surviving members from the 1934 team. Monti was gone, replaced by Andreolo from Uruguay. Gone too was the great goalkeeper Combi, but his shoes were amply filled by Olivieri. And 1938 witnessed the launching of the career of the brilliant goal-making machine named Silvio Piola, who would become Italy's most prolific scorer, surpassing Meazza in 1951.

The four British associations were still split from FIFA. They were invited but refused. Nazi occupation of Austria crushed that country's hopes of competing. The Germans recruited several fine Austria players for their team. Spain was in the midst of its Civil War; Argentina suddenly withdrew, leaving Brazil the sole South American representative since Uruguay did not seek representation; and Mexico also withdrew, opening a place for Cuba, which would create a minor sensation at the games.

Distinguished by a plethora of great center forwards (Brazil's Leonidas, who would win the scoring title, Hungary's Sarosi, Norway's Brunylden, Italy's Piola, and the Czech forward Nejedly), the Cup itself was played under the shadow of impending world war.

Once again, the knock-out system was employed, but this time the host and holder teams were given byes to the final rounds. The first round of actual play saw five of the seven games go into extra-time, with two matches (Switzerland v. Germany and Cuba v. Romania) having to be replayed. In the German-Swiss contest, the first game was very physical, capped by a head goal by Abegglen of Switzerland, who had limped onto the field after being injured to tie the game and send it into overtime. Except for the Austrian Pesser, playing for Germany, being red carded, nothing came of the overtime, and a rematch was played five days later. Now *here* was a game. Two first-half goals produced a German 2–0 lead midway through the game, but a quick goal at the start of the second half put Switzerland back into the game. Then the Swiss lost their left wing Abei, and all hope seemed to vanish. But soon after the return of Abei sparked the Swiss team—Bickel shot the equalizer, and Abegglen produced two more for a 4–2 come-from-behind upset victory for Switzerland.

13

Action during the June 19th final between Hungary (in dark jersey) and Italy. Rava of Italy gets in a header.

But the greater upset involved the other replayed first-round game—this between the experienced Romanian team and the unknown Cubans. After a 3–3 opening game, the Cubans shocked everyone by dropping their brilliant goalkeeper Carvajeles, saying his replacement, Ayra, was even better.

Once again, the eventual loser scored first, but Cuba came back to win 2–1. The second goal created some controversy—the French linesman called offsides, but the German referee allowed it.

Italy had won the 1934 Cup, had won the 1936 Olympics, and in their first match were nearly overcome by the Norwegian team. After yielding an early goal by Ferrari, Norway buckled down, tightly covering Piola while Brunylden was just about all that the Italian fullbacks, led by Andreolo, could handle, hitting the post or crossbar three times. Olivieri's brilliance had to be in top form for these Vikings. Eventually Brustad got the equalizer but was denied a possible winning goal just before extra time. In overtime, the Italian team showed their class, Piola scoring on a rebound.

The Dutch-Czech first round also went into overtime, the Czechs prevailing 3–2. France beat Belgium 3–1, and Hungary dispatched the Dutch East Indians 6–0. The final first-round game, between Poland and Brazil, set the stage for scoring heroics. The scene was muddy Strasbourg, and the heroes led by Leonidas, "The Black Diamond," and Ernest Willimowski, the first half witnessing the hat-trick by the Brazilian, the second half by the Pole. The result: 4–4 at game's end and thus into overtime. There, astonishingly, both men got their fourth goals, but Brazil's Romeu got another, and the South American team went on to win 6–5.

In the second round, Sweden outclassed Cuba 8–0, the technically superior Hungarians outlasted Switzerland 2–0, and the host French team, gambling everything on the attack, could not contain Italy's Piola, losing 3–1.

The final match in these quarter finals, between Czechoslovakia and Brazil, became one of the great World Cup disgraces, ranking alongside the Hungary-Brazil "Battle of Berne" in 1954. Two Brazilians and one Czech were red carded in the match. Planicka, the Czech goalkeeper, broke his arm, and Nejedly, the great Czech goalmaker, his leg.

This disgraceful exhibition began with an early and violent kick of Nejedly by Zeze, who was red carded for it. Nejedly stayed in to equalize on a penalty kick the goal of Leonidas. That was the scoring.

The fighting was another matter. Just before halftime, Riha of Czechoslovakia and Machados of Brazil were sent off for fighting. Two great Czech players were carried off the field, and the game ended in a draw between the nine of Brazil and the depleted ten of Czechoslovakia.

The replay was more like soccer, less like war. Brazil had made nine changes and the Czechs six in order to field their teams. Czechoslovakia led the way with an early goal by Kopecky, only to lose him before the half to injury. In the second half, Leonidas equalized and Roberto volleyed in the winner.

The semifinals produced some surprises. Sweden scored within the first minute of play against Hungary, but then must have rested, as the Hungarians attacked mercilessly, scoring five goals. The Brazilians, meanwhile, decided to rest Leonidas and Tim for the finals, but the gamble proved fruitless as Italy defeated them on a penalty kick by Meazza, 2–1.

The final, played in Stade Colombes in Paris, opened with a classic Italian breakaway after six minutes, Biavati running almost the length of the field before centering it to Meazza, who passed to the scorer

Colaussi. Within a minute Hungary had equalized with Sarosi passing to the unmarked Titkos. Two more goals by Italy seemed to spell the end for Hungary, but Sarosi came back for one more. The scoring was completed with a final goal for Piola, making the score 4–2.

Italy's victory in 1938 was more convincing and less political than her show in 1934. The World Cup had been firmly established as a sporting event rivaling the Olympics. But 1938 would be the last Cup for a dozen years as war and the rebuilding of Europe held off the games until 1950.

1938 (France)

FIRST ROUND

Swtzrlnd (1)(1)**1**
(Abegglen)
Switzerland (0)**4**
(Wallaschek, Bickel, Abegglen 2)
Cuba (0)(2)**3**
(Tunas, Maquina, Sosa)
Cuba (2)**2**
(Socorro, Maquina)
Hungary
(4)**6**
(Kohut, Toldi, Sarosi 2, Zsengeller 2)
France (2)**3**
(Vienante, Nicolas 2)
Czech (0)(0)**3**
(Kostalek, Boucek, Nejedly)

Germany (0)(1)**1**
(Gauchel)
Germany (2)**2**
(Hahnemann, Loertscher, o.g.)
Romania (1)(2)**3**
(Covaci, Baratki, Dobai)
Romania (1)**1**
(Dobai)
Dutch E. Indies
(0)**0**

Belgium (1)**1**
(Isemborghs)
Nethrlnds (0)(0)**0**

Brazil (3)(4)**6**
(Leonidas 4, Peracio, Romeu)
Italy (1)(1)**2**
(Ferrari, Piola)

SECOND ROUND

Sweden (4)**8**
(Andersson, Jonasson, Wetterstroem 4, Nyberg, Keller)
Hungary (1)**2**
(Zsengeller 2)
Italy (1)**3**
(Colaussi, Piola 2)
Brazil (1)(1)**1**
(Leonidas)
Brazil (0)**2**
(Leonidas, Roberto)

SEMIFINALS

Italy (2)**2**
(Colaussi, Meazza*)

Poland (1)(4)**5**
(Willimowski 4, Piontek)
Norway (0)(1)**1**
(Brustad)

Cuba (0)**0**

Switzerland (0)**0**

France (1)**1**
(Heisserer)
Czech (0)(1)**1**
(Nejedly*)
Czech (1)**1**
(Kopecky)

Brazil (0)**1**
(Romeu)

Hungary (3)**5**
(Zsengeller 3, Titkos, Sarosi)
Sweden (1)**1**
(Nyberg)

THIRD PLACE GAME (Bordeaux)

Brazil (1)**4**
(Romeu, Leonidas 2, Peracio)
Sweden (2)**2**
(Jonasson, Nyberg)

FINAL (Paris, 6/19/38)

Italy (3)**4**
(Colaussi 2, Piola 2)
Hungary (1)**2**
(Titkos, Sarosi)

Italy: Olivieri; Foni, Rava; Serantoni, Andreolo, Locatelli; Biavati, Meazza, Piola, Ferrari, Colaussi
Hungary: Szabo; Polger, Biro; Szalay, Szucs, Lazar; Sas, Vincze, Sarosi, Zsengeller, Titkos

Referee: Capdeville (France)

*Penalty kick goal

The Fourth World Cup
Brazil, 1950

sites: Rio de Janeiro, Belo
Horizonte, Porto Alegre, Sao
Paulo, Curitiba
28 entrants; FIFA membership 68

format: 4 groups—winners go to final
pool (which is round robin)

No World Cup games were played in
1942 or 1946 because of World War II.
When Cup play resumed in 1950, FIFA
membership had grown, but the
entrants were down. Germany was still
barred. Hungary, Czechoslovakia,
France, Argentina, the Soviet Union,
and Austria chose not to compete. Part
of the blame for this could be laid at
the feet of the host country, Brazil,
which scheduled the various teams,
except its own, to travel great distances

Stan Mortensen of England gives England her first of two goals in her opening-round
shutout of Chile, heading the ball home from a pass from teammate Mullen (not shown).
The other English player is Finney, and the Chilean is Roldan.

17

Action during the famous U.S.-England contest in which the last-ranked Americans stunned the soccer world by beating England 1–0. Here British keeper Bert Williams makes a save during one of the American attacks on goal.

to stadia all over the country, going from muggy Rio to mountainous Bello Horizonte (the idea of playing each group at one venue was not yet established). Moreover, the strange format—never before used—and the chaotic organization led to last-minute withdrawals. But Uruguay, which sat out the 1934 and 1938 games played in Europe, felt secure enough to come. And, for the first time, England entered the finals—and with an excellent team that was considered cofavorites with Brazil.

The hosts had done as best it could in preparing its country and its team for the games. It had built (actually, it

had not quite completed it by the time the games had begun) what to this day is the largest stadium in the world. Maracana Stadium in Rio holds 200,000 spectators, separated from the pitch by a moat three meters wide and three across. As for its team—Brazil cloistered them in a house outside Rio complete with doctors, masseurs, and chefs.

England had come to play, however, and brought great talent the likes of Tom Finney, Stanley Matthews, Alf Ramsey, Wilf Mannion, and goalkeeper Bert Williams—but no doctor, masseur, or chef. Italy needed more than chefs and doctors. Though they gamely came to defend their title, their chances had really died the year before when a Superba jet carrying the talented Turin team crashed outside Turin, killing seventeen international players. Their famed coach, Vittorio Pozzo, was gone too. Italy's time had passed.

The thirteen teams that made the final were broken up unevenly into four groups. From each group would emerge one team that would go into a final pool, which would play a round robin for the Cup. In Group 1, Brazil disposed of Mexico 4–0 in the opening salvo, and Yugoslavia had followed up with an impressive 3–0 win over Switzerland. So it was eye-opening to see Brazil struggling for a 2–2 draw with the Swiss. Brazil was then in a position of having to beat Yugoslavia to qualify, which they did 2–0.

In Group 3, holders Italy bowed to the superior Swedes and their great center forward, Hans Jeppson. Sweden then merely had to tie Paraguay to qualify. Group 4 was but Uruguay and Bolivia, and the 1930 Cup winners blew the Bolivians away 8–0.

It was Group 2 that provided most of the opening-round thrills. Here England was the favorite, America provided the excitement, and Spain emerged the victor. England opened in sticky Rio, handing Chile a 2–0 loss. But the thin air of Belo Horizonte did not seem to suit the English much better. For this was the setting for America's greatest triumph in World Cup play, a great 1–0 victory over the strong English team—rated by many as the soccer shock of the century. America's underrated team had provided good competition to Spain

earlier, leading 1–0 at the half before losing 3–1. But England was mighty indeed, and no one had seriously given the U.S. much of a chance. Matt Bahr's cross to the head of the Haitian Gaetjens was the sole score of the day. Now England would have to beat Spain in Rio to survive to the final pool. Both sides had beaten Chile 2–0 (and Chile later disposed of the U.S. team by a 5–2 score). England made several lineup changes for its match with Spain, but to no avail. A disallowed goal by Milburn and a second-half goal by Spain's Zarra proved the undoing of England.

So it would be Brazil, Spain, Sweden, and Uruguay for the final pool. After Uruguay and Spain fought to a 2–2 standstill, Brazil rolled over Sweden 7–1, scoring champ Ademir getting four goals. Meanwhile, Uruguay outlasted Sweden 3–2, and Brazil again showed incredible strength as they demolished the well-thought-of Spanish team 6–1. Although it didn't matter for the final, Sweden then beat Spain 3–1. So it turned out that the last-played game would actually be between the top two teams—a game for the championship between what appeared to be the irresistible Brazilians and the stubborn, but as-yet untested Uruguayans.

Nearly 200,000 people jammed Maracana Stadium for the match. Brazil needed only to draw for the Cup championship. Two of the previous three World Cups had been won by the home team. The smart money was on Brazil.

And the Brazilians shone brightly during the first half, but Uruguay's defense toughened for the onslaught, and it was not until the second half that Brazil's Friaca scored. Uruguay's center half Varela then marshaled his troops, and twenty minutes into the second half passed to Ghiggia down the right wing, who centered to the unmarked Schiaffino, who equalized.

Then, with eleven minutes to go, Ghiggia took a pass on the wing, cut in and scored past the near post for the victorious goal. After sitting out two World Cups, Uruguay had come back to play.

1950 (Brazil)

GROUP 1

Brazil (1)**4** **Mexico** (0)**0**
(Ademir 2, Jair, Baltazar)

Yugoslavia (3)**3** **Switzerlnd** (0)**0**
(Tomasevic 2, Ognanov)

Yugoslavia (2)**4** **Mexico** (0)**1**
(Bobek, Cajkow- (Casarin)
ski II 2, Tomasevic)

Brazil (1)**2** **Switzerland** (1)**2**
(Alfredo, Baltazar) (Fatton, Tamini)

Brazil (1)**2** **Yugoslavia** (0)**0**
(Ademir, Zizinho)

Switzerlnd (2)**2** **Mexico** (0)**1**
(Bader, Fatton) (Velasquez)

	GP	W	D	L	GF	GA	Pts
Brazil	3	2	1	0	8	2	5
Yugoslavia	3	2	0	1	7	3	4
Switzerland	3	1	1	1	4	6	3
Mexico	3	0	0	3	2	10	0

GROUP 2

Spain (0)**3** **USA** (1)**1**
(Basora 2, Zarra) (Souza, J.)

England (1)**2** **Chile** (0)**0**
(Mortensen, Man-
nion)

USA (1)**1** **England** (0)**0**
(Gaetjens)

Spain (2)**2** **Chile** (0)**0**
(Basora, Zarra)

Spain (0)**1** **England** (0)**0**
(Zarra)

Chile (2)**5** **USA** (0)**2**
(Robledo, Crema- (Pariani, Souza, J.)
schi 3, Prieto)

	GP	W	D	L	GF	GA	Pts
Spain	3	3	0	0	6	1	6
England	3	1	0	2	2	2	2
Chile	3	1	0	2	5	6	2
USA	3	1	0	2	4	8	2

GROUP 3

Sweden (2)**3** **Italy** (1)**2**
(Jeppson 2, Anders- (Carapellese, Muc-
son) cinelli)

Sweden (2)**2** **Paraguay** (1)**2**
(Sundqvist, Palmer) (Lopez, A.,
Lopez, F.)

Italy (1)**2** **Paraguay** (0)**0**
(Carapellese,
Pandolfini)

	GP	W	D	L	GF	GA	Pts
Sweden	2	1	1	0	5	4	3
Italy	2	1	0	1	4	3	2
Paraguay	2	0	1	1	2	4	1

GROUP 4

Uruguay (4)**8** **Bolivia** (0)**0**
(Schiaffino 4, Mi-
guez 2, Vidal,
Ghiggia)

	GP	W	D	L	GF	GA	Pts
Uruguay	1	1	0	0	8	0	2
Bolivia	1	0	0	1	0	8	0

FINAL POOL

Uruguay (1)**2** **Spain** (2)**2**
(Ghiggia, Varela) (Basora 2)

Brazil (3)**7** **Sweden** (0)**1**
(Ademir 4, Chico 2, (Andersson*)
Maneca)

Uruguay (1)**3** **Sweden** (2)**2**
(Ghiggia, Miguez 2) (Palmer, Sundqvist)

Brazil (3)**6** **Spain** (0)**1**
(Jair 2, Chico 2, (Igoa)
Zizinho, Parra,
o.g.)

Sweden (2)**3** **Spain** (0)**1**
(Johnsson, Mell- (Zarra)
berg, Palmer)

Uruguay (0)**2** **Brazil** (0)**1**
(Schiaffino, Ghiggia) (Friaca)

(Deciding match played at Rio de Janeiro, 7/16/50)

	GP	W	D	L	GF	GA	Pts
Uruguay	3	2	1	0	7	5	5
Brazil	3	2	0	1	14	4	4
Sweden	3	1	0	0	6	11	2
Spain	3	0	1	2	4	11	1

Uruguay: Maspoli; Gonzales, Tejera; Gam-
bretta, Varela, Andrade; Ghiggia, Perez,
Miguez, Schiaffino, Moran
Brazil: Barbosa; Augusto, Juvenal; Bauer,
Banilo, Bigode; Friaca, Zizinho, Ademir, Jair,
Chico

*Penalty kick goal

Referee: Reader (England)

The Fifth World Cup
Switzerland, 1954

sites: Lausanne, Geneva, Zurich, Berne, Basel, Lugano
36 entrants, FIFA membership 80

format: 4 groups, each advancing 2 to a quarterfinal that would utilize knock-out (single elimination) thereafter

By 1954, the World Cup championships had stood Italy 2, Uruguay 2, the rest of the world 0. But all that was to change. Since the 1950 games, these two champions have not repeated, although Italy reached the finals in

England's Broadis jumps over the outstretched leg of Martinez of Uruguay during quarterfinal action in which the South American team beat England 4–2.

1970. Italy didn't make the quarterfinals in 1954 and were eliminated in 1958 before making the final sixteen. Eliminated again in 1962, they were embarrassed by the North Koreans, 1–0, in 1966, an upset that ranks in World Cup lore with America's 1950 1–0 victory over England. The poor Italian team was met by thousands of spectators at the airport and bombarded with eggs. In 1970, Italy lost the final to Brazil, and in 1974 and 1978 showed little.

Uruguay, considered the most powerful South American team during the fifties, has become an also-ran since then. After falling to Hungary in the semifinals in 1954, it failed to qualify in 1958 and has shown little in subsequent Cups. Uruguay since the beginning has been the victim of scouting raids by other countries. This, coupled with the fact that their principal talent seems to come from two powerful teams, Nacional and Penarol, which oftentimes would not release their international players for World Cup competition, has led to the demise of Uruguay's prominence.

Nineteen fifty-four marked the beginning of modern soccer's development. During the next twenty

More action from the quarterfinal match between England and Uruguay. Finney and Lofthouse of England are shown in action in front of the Uruguay goal. But it wasn't enough as Uruguay knocked Britain out of the tourney.

years, we would see more players involved in the attack and more freedom of movement for defenders. The attacking sweeper was created, exemplified by Italy's Giacinto Facchetti and, especially, West Germany's incomparable Franz Beckenbauer. Brazil became the model for the world during this period—at one time winning three out of four World Cups after losing at home in 1950.

But in 1954 the emerging power was Hungary. As seen later during the 1970s with the Netherlands, a small country can produce a uniquely talented generation of players who dominate the game for a while and whose style of play is emulated by others. Hungary was such a country; 1954 was such a year.

The Hungarians massacred the English team on British soil the year before, 6–3 and 7–1. They had a devastating attack, led by captain Ferenc Puskas, whose left foot was practically a lethal weapon, striking fear in the hearts of even the most gallant goalkeeper. Puskas led a team full of world-class attackers—Czibor, Kocsis, Hidegkuti, and Boszik. They had come to rule.

Other countries of note included Austria, led by halfback Ernest Ocwirk; Brazil, with a strong right side in Julinho and Didi and a fine pair of fullbacks, Nilton and Djalma Santos; and Yugoslavia, with veteran forwards Mitic and Bobek, plus new scorers Zebec, Vukas, and Milutinovic. Italy brought its defense-minded team formed around the Inter Milan *bloc*. A bloc is a system in which a pool of players from one team are selected for a national team, occasionally employed by national teams to provide a cohesive unit around which to play (the U.S. isn't the only national team to have only a month or so preparation time).

The format was odd in that there were only two games for each four-team pool—rather than a three-game round robin. This had the effect of having some of the stronger teams within the same pool not playing against each other in the opening rounds; and some of the weak sisters were blown out—Brazil beat Mexico 5–0, Hungary crushed South Korea 9–0, West Germany polished off Turkey 4–1 and 7–2 without extending itself, Uruguay destroyed Scotland 7–0.

In Group 1, Yugoslavia's 1–0 win over France was a mild upset to this odd pool system, and Yugoslavia advanced to the quarterfinals along with Brazil, against which it had played a fine 1–1 standoff.

Group 2 produced lopsided scores and the psychological victory of West Germany, orchestrated by its brilliant manager, Sepp Herberger. Germany had beaten the Turks handily 4–1, and Hungary had overwhelmed the South Koreans. To advance to the quarterfinals, Germany need not beat the elegant Hungarians, Herberger rightly saw—only not lose the inevitable playoff against Turkey again since it was likely the Turks would beat the Koreans. So Germany started a team of reserves against the onrushing Hungarians, who trounced them 8–3. The rest of the scenerio was played out, and the Germans accompanied Hungary to the quarterfinals.

Group 3 did as they were predicted (the only one, I might add) by having the two strong sides defeat the two weak ones—Austria and Uruguay over Scotland and Czechoslovakia. Scotland fought gamely against the Austrians (who were saved from overtime by their brilliant goalie, Schmied) only to be taken apart by Uruguay.

Group 4 produced the most interesting games, with England leading the way by blowing its chance to beat Belgium and having to settle for a 4–4 tie. Switzerland, as with so many World Cup hosts, played above itself and beat Italy in the main early-round upset of the games, although the Brazilian referee allowed the game to degenerate into name calling and gratuitous fouls and received for his efforts a chase off the field by the hot-blooded Lorenzi after disallowing an Italian goal. England then overcame Switzerland 2–0, and Italy beat Belgium 4–1, producing a tie for second place between Switzerland and Italy. Their rematch produced none of the difficulties of their first game, with the enthusiastic Swiss, cheered on by their fans, handing the superior Italians a 4–1 loss.

The four quarterfinal games averaged over six goals apiece, although the first was a 2–0 West German win over Yugoslavia that was even closer than the score would indicate. The Yugoslavs dominated play for over half the game and scored the first goal on themselves, the defender Horvat sending a back pass into the nets. Germany's fullback Kohnmeyer made three goal-line clearances before German winger Helmut Rahn scored the second goal.

The Austrian-Swiss quarterfinal was even better—a twelve goal back-and-forth battle, eventually won by Austria 7–5. The Swiss, with their famous "Swiss Bolt" strategy, took a three-goal lead, but Austria, shooting from long range, made up the difference in an amazing three minutes, then added two more before the Swiss produced its fourth—all this in the first half alone. A great game.

England lost to Uruguay 4–2 in a game noted mainly for an inept play by English goalkeeper Merrick in clearing a shot off the foot of Schiaffino after Uruguay's Varela took a free kick illegally by kicking it from his hands as it dropped.

Which brings us to one of the most notorious World Cup games ever played—the "Battle of Berne" between Hungary and Brazil. The violence started early and continued even after the game. Forty-two free kicks were awarded, two penalty kicks, four men were cautioned, and three were red carded. Here's the blow-by-blow.

Hungary took an early lead when Hidegkuti outfoxed the Brazilian goalie and scored, getting his shorts ripped off in the process. Meanwhile Hungary's Lorant contemptuously laughed in the face of English ref Arthur Ellis after being cautioned. At the eighth minute Kocsis, known as "the Golden Head," used it to put Hungary up by two. The violence and retaliation increased, and just before halftime a penalty shot by Djalma Santos brought Brazil back into the game.

After halftime came a crucial decision, resulting in a questionable penalty shot for Hungary. It occurred after Kocsis collided with Santos and another defender fell during the mixup, possibly touching the ball with his arms. Both sides apparently expected a free kick for Brazil, but Ellis instead awarded a penalty shot on the basis of the hand ball. Now it was 3–1, Hungary.

Brazil's Julinho's fine goal brought it back to 3–2; then the fight began. Nilton Santos and Boszik started in and were sent off, but police were needed to escort them off the field. Then Djalma Santos chased Czibor, who had filled in brilliantly for the injured Puskas, all over the field. Later Humberto Tozzi kicked a Hungarian player and was sent off—but not before falling to his knees and pleading with Ellis to allow him to stay. Kocsis then added a fourth goal before the whistle.

But the Brazilians' discontent spilled over after the game as well; they hid in the tunnel leading to the locker rooms, turned out the lights, and waited for the victorious Hungarians. The ensuing fight in the Hungarian locker room produced several casualties but no change of score. The Brazilian federation took strong measures in disciplining its players.

The semifinals were happier events. In fact, the Lausanne match between Hungary and Uruguay is regarded as one of the finest in World Cup history. Trailing 2–0 with less than fifteen minutes left, Argentine-born Hohberg scored twice for Uruguay (almost three times—his third shot hit the post) on passes from Schiaffino, who then was injured. The brilliant Kocsis quickly added goals #2 and #3 of the day, and Hungary won 4–2. Incredibly, it was Uruguay's first World Cup defeat.

The other semifinal saw Germany outclass Austria 6–1, scoring five goals in the second half. Austria overcame the favored Uruguayans for the third-place consolation match 3–1.

The final in Berne, like the "Battle" earlier, was played in a driving rain. Puskas was finally back, though not at 100 percent. But enough, as he collected the first goal on a rebound off the shot of Kocsis. Two minutes later, and it was 2–0; it looked to be a repeat of the earlier trouncing Hungary had laid on Germany.

But the Germans were not finished and fought back gamely. Within three minutes Morlock scored, and soon thereafter came the equalizer from Rahn—and it stood tied at the half.

The form of Germany's Turek at goal combined with the missed chances of Puskas and the bad luck of several other Hungarian front runners (Hidegkuti and Kocsis had both hit the woodwork) to keep the standoff thrilling. Then with fifteen minutes to go, Rahn scored his second goal—this from fifteen yards out. It was now 3–2, Germany. Puskas's offside goal from Toth's pass was disallowed, and Turek made a great save of Czibor's shot in the dying seconds of play. The wily Herberger, the father of modern soccer in Germany, had pulled off an upset over the superior Hungarians. The Germans would do the same against the equally superior Dutch twenty years later. Hungary's incredible team came within a hairsbreath . . . and lost. Within two years, the Red Army would be in Budapest, and Hungary's greatness would be gone.

1954 (Switzerland)

GROUP 1

Yugoslavia (1)1 (Milutinovic)	France (0)0		
Brazil (4)5 (Baltazar, Didi, Pinga 2, Julinho)	Mexico (0)0		
France (1)3 (Vincent, Cardenas, o.g., Kopa*)	Mexico (0)2 (Naranjo, Balcazar)		
Brazil (0)(1)1 (Didi)	Yugoslv (0)(1)1 (Zebec)		

	GP	W	D	L	GF	GA	Pts
Brazil	2	1	1	0	6	1	3
Yugoslavia	2	1	1	0	2	1	3
France	2	1	0	1	3	3	2
Mexico	2	0	0	2	2	8	0

GROUP 2

Hungary (4)9 (Czibor, Kocsis 3, Puskas 2, Lantos, Palotas 2)	Rep. Korea (0)0
German FR (1)4 (Klodt, Morlock, Schaefer, Walter, O.)	Turkey (1)1 (Suat)
Hungary (3)8 (Hidegkuti 2, Kocsis 4, Puskas, Toth)	German FR (1)3 (Pfaff, Hermann, Rahn)
Turkey (4)7 (Burhan 3, Erol, Lefter, Suat 2)	Rep. Korea (0)0

	GP	W	D	L	GF	GA	Pts
Hungary	2	2	0	0	17	3	4
German FR	2	1	0	1	7	9	2
Turkey	2	1	0	1	8	4	2
Rep. Korea	2	0	0	2	0	16	0

PLAYOFF

German FR (3)7 (Morlock 3, Walter, O., Walter, F., Schaefer 2)	Turkey (1)2 (Mustafa, Lefter)

GROUP 3

Austria (1)1 (Probst)	Scotland (0)0
Uruguay (0)2 (Miguez, Schiaffino)	Czech (0)0
Austria (4)5 (Stojaspal 2, Probst 3)	Czech (0)0
Uruguay (2)7 (Borges 3, Miguez 2, Abbadie 2)	Scotland (0)0

	GP	W	D	L	GF	GA	Pts
Uruguay	2	2	0	0	9	0	4
Austria	2	2	0	0	6	0	4
Czechoslovakia	2	0	0	2	0	7	0
Scotland	2	0	0	2	0	8	0

GROUP 4

England (2)(3)4 (Broadis 2, Lofthouse 2)	Belgium (1)(3)4 (Anoul 2, Coppens, Dickinson, o.g.)
Switzerland (1)2 (Ballaman, Hugi)	Italy (1)1 (Boniperti)
England (1)2 (Mullen, Wilshaw)	Switzerland (0)0
Italy (1)4 (Pandolfini*, Galli, Frignani, Lorenzi)	Belgium (0)1 (Anoul)

	GP	W	D	L	GF	GA	Pts
England	2	1	1	0	6	4	3
Switzerland	2	1	0	1	2	3	2
Italy	2	1	0	1	2	3	2
Belgium	2	0	1	1	5	8	1

PLAYOFF

Switzerlnd (1)4 (Hugi 2, Ballaman, Fatton)	Italy (0)1 (Nesti)

QUARTERFINALS

German FR (1)2 (Horvat, o.g., Rahn)	Yugoslavia (0)0
Hungary (2)4 (Hidegkuti, Kocsis 2, Lantos*)	Brazil (1)2 (Santos, D.*, Julinho)
Austria (5)7 (Koerner, A. 2, Ocwirk, Wagner 3, Probst)	Switzerland (4)5 (Ballaman 2, Hugi 2, Hanappi, o.g.)
Uruguay (2)4 (Borges, Varela, Schiaffino, Ambrois)	England (1)2 (Lofthouse, Finney)

SEMIFINALS

German FR (1)6 (Schaefer, Morlock, Walter, F. 2**, Walter, O. 2)	Austria (0)1 (Probst)
Hungary (1)(2)4 (Czibor, Hidegkuti, Kocsis 2)	Uruguay (0)(2)2 (Hohberg 2)

THIRD PLACE GAME

Austria (1)3 (Stojaspal*, Cruz, o.g., Ocwirk)	Uruguay (1)1 (Hohberg)

FINAL (Berne, 7/4/54)

German FR (2)3 (Morlock, Rahn 2)	Hungary (2)2 (Puskas, Czibor)

German Federal Republic: Turek; Posipal, Kohlmeyer; Eckel, Liebrich, Mai; Rahn, Morlock, Walter, O., Walter, F., Schaefer

Hungary: Grosics; Buzansky, Lantos; Bozsik, Lorant, Zakarias; Czibor, Kocsis, Hidegkuti, Puskas, Toth

Referee: Ling (England)

*Penalty kick goal

The Sixth World Cup
Sweden, 1958

sites: Malmö, Halmstad, Hälsinborg,
Norrkoping, Vasteras,
Cerebro, Ekilstuna,
Stockholm, Sandviken,
Gothenburg, Boras
53 entrants; FIFA membership 86

format: 4 groups, each advancing 2 to
a quarterfinal that would
utilize knock-out thereafter

After the Hungarian Revolution, Puskas, Kocsis, and Czibor defected to Spain, and the team Hungary brought to Sweden was but a shell of the great 1954 team. The Cup victors, Germany, had basically put together a new team—quite good although not of the level of its 1954 champion. The two other World Cup champions, Uruguay and Italy, were not in the finals at all—both were stopped in their quest for representation by relative unknowns, Paraguay handing Uruguay a 5–0 thrashing and Northern Ireland upsetting the Italians (this despite the loss of key Northern Ireland players from the tragic Munich air crash in February 1958 of a plane carrying the fame Manchester United team—a crash that severely damaged the English World Cup team as well).

Brazil had learned from its 1954 Cup mistakes and its poor showing in the preparation matches in Europe two years later when England beat it 4–2 at Wembley. Didi and Nilton Santos were back, but 1954 was to belong to an unknown seventeen-year-old, Edison Arantes do Nascimento, better known as Pele.

Argentina, winners in 1957 of the South American championship, had had its stars lured away by the Italians and was not really a major threat in 1958.

Britain boasted four finalists— England, Northern Ireland, Scotland, which had eliminated Spain, and the surprising Wales team, which beat Israel in order to fill the slot made by Uruguay's withdrawal. The Welsh were eventually to defeat the Hungarians, draw with Sweden, and lose 1–0 against Brazil—not bad at all.

Sweden had recognized professionalism in athletics and recalled from Italy world-class players who had gone abroad to play. Sweden, playing at home, seemed to grow stronger with each match in the games.

Again, the format was to break the sixteen finalists into four groups with team winners to go to the quarterfinals, after which it would be single elimination. The only difference from the 1954 format was that the pools played round robin rather than just two games.

In Group 1, West Germany lorded it over Argentina 3–1 and Northern

Two photos of the controversial goal
awarded Germany by English referee Ellis in
Germany's match with Czechoslovakia. The
goal resulted when German forward Hans
Schaeffer charged toward the goalie while he
held the ball. The Czechs claim the ball
never crossed the line. The top photo shows
the moment when Schaeffer makes his
move. Photo at right was taken after Ellis
awarded the goal. Goalkeeper Dolejsi holds
the ball while teammate Novak looks very
dejected. The Czechs refused to play in any
game refereed by Ellis after this game. This
first goal was decisive, since the game ended
in a 2–2 draw.

Nils Liedholm (lighter shirt) scores Sweden's first goal during the Cup final against Brazil, which went on to beat Sweden 5–2.

Ireland started out well with a 1–0 victory over the Czechs. But then Argentina beat Northern Ireland, and West Germany drew with both Northern Ireland and Czechoslovakia, which then thrashed Argentina 6–1. Result: each of the four teams won only one game. Northern Ireland and Czechoslovakia, having drawn once each, played for the right to accompany twice-tied Germany— Northern Ireland winning 2–1 (in overtime, naturally).

Group 2's results were more decisive. France unraveled Paraguay 7–3, with Juste Fontaine, who was expected to be a reserve, scoring a hat-trick. Fontaine scored in every game for France, ending the games with thirteen goals, which remains a World Cup record. Scotland, meanwhile, played well in drawing with Yugoslavia 1–1 before losing by single goals to Paraguay and France. The Yugoslavs defeated the French 3–2 and drew with Paraguay 3–3 for the right to accompany France to the quarterfinals.

Sweden opened Group 3 with a victory over Mexico 3–1, followed up with a 2–1 win over Hungary, but had to settle for a scoreless tie with the tough Wales team. Hungary drew with Wales and defeated Mexico 4–0. Since Wales, with three ties, and Hungary, with a win and a tie, both had three qualifying points, they conducted a playoff, won by Wales in a rough game.

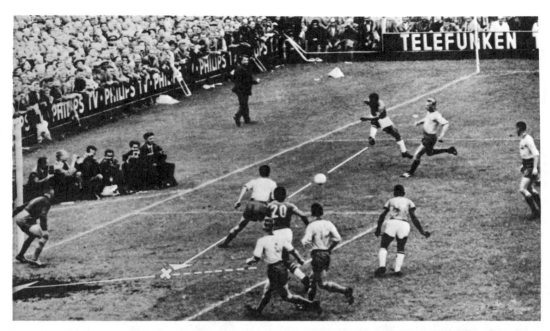

Two views of the same great goal—Brazil's first of five in the World Cup final against Sweden. Shown at top is Garrincha crossing the ball in front of the Swedish goal mouth, where Vava (no. 20) is getting in position to hammer the equalizer home. The white markings show the path of the ball into the net. The lower photo was taken just after Vava one-touched it in past the Swedish goalie Svensson.

The victorious Brazilians after their World Cup final victory. Scoring wizards were Pele (kneeling, 3rd from left) and Vava (kneeling, 4th from left).

Group 4 was by far the toughest pool—Brazil, England, the Soviet Union, and Austria. The Soviets had won the Melbourne Olympics two years earlier and in Lev Yashin had an incomparable goalkeeper. They played to a well-fought 2–2 tie with England. Brazil, without the services of the injured Pele, beat Austria 3–0, two goals coming from nineteen-year-old Jose ("Mazzola") Altafini, who had already been signed by Inter Milan. England then put on a fine show, playing to a scoreless tie with Brazil—the only time Brazil failed to score, but Pele, Zito, and Garrincha didn't play.

England's manager Walter Winterbottom, and assistant, Bill Nicholson, devised a tactical plan to hold back the 4–2–4 Brazilian attack by reshuffling their lineup to leave the Brazilians little room to operate in the buildup phase. This marked the beginning of denying space and marking key players man-to-man (in this case, Bill Slater marked Didi).

The Soviet Union then beat the Austrians and lost to Brazil by identical 2–0 scores, but England couldn't handle the plodding Austrians, drawing 2–2, and thus becoming the third British team to be involved in playoffs, but the only one to lose, succumbing 1–0 to the Soviet Union after England's winger Brabrook hit the post twice before Ilyin shot the winner—ironically it came in off a post.

By the quarterfinals, Northern Ireland had run out of luck, fit players, and steam, losing 4–0 to the French. Yugoslavia dominated its game against West Germany but lost 1–0 on a goal by Rahn. Sweden meanwhile breezed along comfortably against the Soviets 2–0. The game of note was the squeaky win of mighty Brazil over tiny Wales 1–0 on a goalkeeper-deflected goal by Pele, a goal the star has called "the most important goal in my career." Altogether a fine show by the gallant Welshmen.

After thirty-seven minutes of their semifinal match with Brazil in Stockholm, the French lost their superb center half, Bob Jonquet, and their whole defense unraveled. It was tied at 1 apiece then. Within minutes Vava had put Brazil ahead. Fontaine equalized in the second half, but after that it was all Brazil. Didi scored one and assisted two others to Pele, giving the superstar a hat-trick. At the whistle it was 5–2.

The other semifinal was closer. The confident Swedes had the Gothenburg crowd behind them but the determined West German team in front. Early on Germany's center forward Uwe Seeler crossed the ball to the inside left Schaefer, who volleyed it brilliantly into the goal. Five minutes later

Skogland equalized from a sharp angle, and it stood tied at the half.

After three minutes into the half, German fullback Juskowiak gave a slashing foul to Sweden's tricky right wing Kurt Hamrin and was red carded. Another terrible foul—this by Sweden's Parling on Fritz Walter—was not called, and Walter limped throughout the rest of the game. With nine minutes to go, Gren put Sweden ahead, and later Hamrin nailed the coffin shut with another goal.

France, with its remarkable goal-making machine, Fontaine, picking up four, overcame demoralized Germany 6–3 for third place.

Sweden wanted the final's first goal; they knew they would have to attack early to stand a chance against the brilliant front-running Brazilians. They indeed did draw first blood with Liedholm dribbling through Brazil's defense for a score after four minutes. But the South Americans were undeterred. Garrincha set up two early goals for Vava to take the lead 2–1. In the second half, Pele did his magic, scoring a breathtaking juggling goal and heading another. Left wing Zagalo (later to become Brazil's coach) added a fifth while Sweden's Simonsson gave Sweden its second, and the home team went down before the superior Brazilians 5–2. It was to be the first of three World Cup victories for Brazil in four Cups. And it signaled the start of the legend of Pele.

1958 (Sweden)

GROUP 1

German FR (2)3   **Argentina** (1)1
(Rahn 2, Schmidt)   (Corbatta)

N. Ireland (1)1   **Czech** (0)0
(Cush)

German FR (1)2   **Czech** (0)2
(Schaefer, Rahn)   (Dvorak*, Zikan)

Argentina (1)3   **N. Ireland** (1)1
(Corbatta 2*, Me-   (McParland)
nendez)

German FR (1)2   **N. Ireland** (1)2
(Rahn, Seeler)   (McParland 2)

Czech (3)6   **Argentina** (1)1
(Dvorak, Zikan 2,   (Corbatta)
Feureisl, Hovorka 2)

	GP	W	D	L	GF	GA	Pts
German FR	3	1	2	0	7	5	4
Czechoslovakia	3	1	1	1	8	4	3
N. Ireland	3	1	1	1	4	5	3
Argentina	3	1	0	2	5	10	2

PLAYOFF

N. Ireland(1)(1)2   **Czech** (1)(1)1
(McParland 2)   (Zikan)

GROUP 2

France (2)7   **Paraguay** (4)3
(Fontaine 3, Pian-   (Amarilla 2*, Ro-
toni, Kopa, Wis-   mero)
nieski, Vincent)

Yugoslavia (1)1   **Scotland** (0)1
(Petakovic)   (Murray)

Yugoslavia (1)3   **France** (1)2
(Petakovic, Veseli-   (Fontaine 2)
novic 2)

Paraguay (2)3   **Scotland** (1)2
(Aguero, Re, Parodi)   (Mudie, Collins)

France (2)2   **Scotland** (0)1
(Kopa, Fontaine)   (Baird)

Yugoslavia (2)3   **Paraguay** (1)3
(Ognjanovic,   (Parodi, Aguero,
Rajkov,   Romero)
Veselinovic)

*Penalty kick goal

	GP	W	D	L	GF	GA	Pts
France	3	2	0	1	11	7	4
Yugoslavia	3	1	2	0	7	6	4
Paraguay	3	1	1	1	9	12	3
Scotland	3	0	1	2	4	6	1

GROUP 3

Sweden (1)3   **Mexico** (0)0
(Simonsson 2,
Liedholm*)

Hungary (1)1   **Wales** (1)1
(Bozsik)   (Charles, J.)

Wales (1)1   **Mexico** (1)1
(Allchurch)   (Belmonte)

Sweden (1)2   **Hungary** (0)1
(Hamrin 2)   (Tichy)

Hungary (1)4   **Mexico** (0)0
(Tichy 2, Sandor,
Bencsics)

Sweden (0)0   **Wales** (0)0

	GP	W	D	L	GF	GA	Pts
Sweden	3	2	1	0	5	1	5
Wales	3	0	3	0	2	2	3
Hungary	3	1	1	1	6	3	3
Mexico	3	0	1	2	1	8	1

PLAYOFF

Wales (0)2   **Hungary** (0)1
(Allchurch, Medwin)   (Tichy)

GROUP 4

England (0)2   **USSR** (1)2
(Kevan, Finney*)   (Simonian, Ivanov,
   A.)

Brazil (1)3   **Austria** (0)0
(Mazzola 2,
Santos, N.)

England (0)0   **Brazil** (0)0

USSR (1)2   **Austria** (0)0
(Ilyin, Ivanov, V.)

Brazil (1)2   **USSR** (0)0
(Vava 2)

England (0)2   **Austria** (1)2
(Haynes, Kevan)   (Koller, Koerner)

	GP	W	D	L	GF	GA	Pts
Brazil	3	2	1	0	5	0	5
USSR	3	1	1	1	4	4	3
England	3	0	3	0	4	4	3
Austria	3	0	1	2	2	7	1

PLAYOFF

USSR (0)1   **England** (0)0
(Ilyin)

QUARTERFINALS

France (1)4   **N. Ireland** (0)0
(Wisnieski, Fon-
taine 2, Piantoni)

German FR (1)1   **Yugoslavia** (0)0
(Rahn)

Sweden (0)2   **USSR** (0)0
(Hamrin, Simonsson)

Brazil (0)1   **Wales** (0)0
(Pele)

SEMIFINALS

Brazil (2)5   **France** (1)2
(Vava, Didi,   (Fontaine, Pian-
Pele 3)   toni)

Sweden (1)3   **German FR** (1)1
(Skoglund, Gren,   (Schaefer)
Hamrin)

THIRD PLACE TEAM (Gothenburg)

France (0)6   **German FR** (0)3
(Fontaine 4, Kopa*,   (Cieslarczyk,
Douis)   Rahn, Schaefer)

FINAL (Stockholm, 6/29/58)

Brazil (2)5   **Sweden** (1)2
(Vava 2, Pele 2,   (Liedholm, Simons-
Zagalo)   son)

Brazil: Gylmar; Santos, D., Santos, N.;
Zito, Bellini, Orlando; Garrincha, Didi, Vava,
Pele, Zagalo
Sweden: Svensson; Bergmark, Axbom;
Boerjesson, Gustavsson, Parling; Hamrin,
Gren, Simonsson, Liedholm, Skoglund

Referee: Guigue (France)

The Seventh World Cup
Chile, 1962

sites: Arica, Santiago, Vina del Mar, Rancagua

57 entrants; FIFA membership 104

format: 4 groups (goal average to decide ties, not playoffs), each advancing 2 to quarterfinals that utilize knock-out thereafter

Because rather than despite a series of devastating earthquakes suffered by Chile, FIFA decided compassionately/ controversially to award the games to that South American country. Chile built a new stadium in Santiago to hold the final, charged incredible ticket prices, and generally did a pretty good job of organizing.

But this was not to prove an exciting World Cup for the fans. It marked the beginning of defense-dominated soccer—there were nearly twice as many matches with one or

Mexico's Sepulveda heads the ball away from Brazil's Djalma (right) and Zito (no. 5) as Hernandez (no. 9) backs up the play during early play. Brazil had an unexpectedly difficult time, beating Mexico 2–0.

West Germany's Uwe Seeler heads home in play action against Chile as Navarro (left) and Sanchez, both beaten, look on. Germany went on to win 2–0 to go through to the quarterfinals.

fewer goals as there were those with five or more. And compare the scoring title of five goals by Yugoslavia's Jerkovic, accomplished with Juste Fontaine's total of thirteen just four years before.

South America had five finalists— Brazil (as World Cup holder, it was an automatic entry), Chile (as host, also automatic), Uruguay, Argentina, and Colombia. Mexico represented CONCACAF; Eastern Europe sent Hungary, Yugoslavia, Czechoslovakia, Bulgaria, and the USSR; and Western Europe was represented by only five teams—West Germany, Switzerland, England, Italy, and Spain, the two last-named entrants being full of Latin American players (on Italy, Altafini and Sivori; on Spain, Santamaria and diStefano as well as the great Hungarian Puskas, although two Brazilian players, Didi and Vava,

played with their home teams, having been given permission by their parent club, Real Madrid of Spain).

Among the formidable lineups, one must include the Soviet Union (having recently beaten Argentina, Uruguay, and Chile). Otherwise, it seemed headed toward being pretty much a South American affair. Soccer dominance had clearly moved there. England had recently dropped a match to Scotland (the first time in a quarter century), Hungary was still in a tailspin, and Germany was without the incomparable Fritz Walter to form a team around.

Group 1 provided some chills, upsets, and near upsets as Colombia surprised everyone—first scaring Uruguay by leading at half only to lose 2–1, then shocking the Soviets by coming back from a 3–1 deficit to tie 4–4. The Soviet goalie Yashin,

Top photo shows Switzerland's Eisener making a desperate save as Sivori of Italy jumps over during early play. Italy won 3–0. Photo on the right occurred during quarterfinal play between England and Brazil. Vava heads the ball past England's goalie Ron Springett for the second goal in Brazil's 3–1 victory.

played terribly, letting in a goal directly from a corner and failing to stop even routine shots.

But before all this, the Soviets and the Yugoslavs had it out with each other, meeting in a brutal confrontation noted for its turn-the-other-cheek refereeing (which was just as well, since Yugoslavia's Jerkovic aimed a blow at the aforesaid cheek— without being red carded). It took

Yugoslavia's team manager to send Mujic home after the latter broke the leg of Soviet fullback Dubinski (the ref did nothing). Incredibly, no one was sent off the field (though a few were carried off). But in this battle, Yashin shone, and the Soviets won 2–0. Both the USSR and Yugoslavia beat Uruguay, and in the final match the Yugoslavs overpowered failing Colombia to go through to the quarterfinals with the Soviets.

Group 2 provided fewer thrills—but only just. The relatively calm games and close scores (Germany beating Chile 2–0 and drawing scoreless with Italy; and everybody beating hapless Switzerland) were overshadowed by a disgraceful brawl between Italy and Chile, apparently triggered by articles appearing in Italian newspapers criticizing the way of life in Chile and expressing disappointment that the Italian team had to play under such poverty-stricken conditions. Chile's team took offense, and their normally physical style of play guaranteed that Italy would find out of their displeasure. Inevitably, Italy retaliated. The results speak for themselves—two Italians, fullback David and inside left Ferrini, were carded and departed, and inside right Maschio had his nose broken in a famous, well-televised left hook that the English ref, Ken Aston, alone in the stadium (and perhaps the world) seemed to have missed. Playing shortsided with nine players took its toll on the Italians, and two second-half goals won it for the home team, which accompanied West Germany to the quarterfinals.

Brazil's 2–0 debut against Mexico included a second-half score by Pele, remarkable only in that it was his sole goal of the Cup, since he severely pulled a leg muscle in Brazil's next Group 3 game, a scoreless tie with Czechoslovakia, and spent the rest of the Cup in the whirlpool and with ice packs. Heroics would have to come elsewhere for Brazil. And they did, principally in the person of Garrincha, who had one leg shorter than the other, making him an unpredictable dribbler, with amazing pace and agility, deadly with foot or head, and a free kick specialist to boot. Garrincha's second-half passes to Pele's replacement, Amarildo, provided Brazil's two goals to overcome a young but determined Spanish team's halftime 1–0 lead. Czechoslovakia's defeat of Spain led to its inclusion, with Brazil, in the quarterfinals.

Hungary and England went through from Group 4, Hungary on the strength of its 2–1 win over England and a 6–1 stomping of Bulgaria; and England, though it was tied with Argentina with a victory, a draw, and a loss, advanced on the basis of goal average, having defeated Argentina 3–1 and drawing scoreless with Bulgaria while the South Americans drew with Hungary and beat Bulgaria in the opener by only 1–0.

The quarterfinals saw a gallant English team take on mighty Brazil and but for a poor performance by keeper Springett, who dropped a swerving free kick by Garrincha, allowing Vava to score, might have come through better. Garrincha himself scored two goals (head and boot), to give Brazil a 3–1 margin.

The Chileans, on paper, were long on home-team support and short on talent, but they disposed of the Soviets, Yashin having his second poor showing, being deceived by Leonel Sanchez's free kick and then was completely beaten by Eladio Rojas's booming thirty-five yarder.

Even though Czechoslovakia had managed to win but one game (and that a not-overwhelming victory over Spain by 1–0), they needed only one on a breakaway by inside right Scherer to contain the Hungarians, albeit with the brilliant play of keeper Schroiff plus a little luck from the posts that kept getting in the way of Hungarian shots.

Now the moment of truth for Chile—in the big-time semifinals with the big-time Brazilians. Again the irrepressible Garrincha added the excitement with a twenty-yard shot, a head goal from the corner, and a great corner to the head of Vava (who later provided another head goal).

Meanwhile, dark-horse Czechoslovakia overcame Yugoslavia 3–1 before a mere 5,000 spectators in Vina del Mar (all other eyes were on the Chile-Brazil contest). Goalie Schroiff was again the hero.

In the final, Czechoslovakia shocked the champion Brazilians early on with a beautiful goal by Masapust off the pass of Scherer. But keeper Schroiff, so brilliant before, had finally come up empty, allowing a narrow-angle equalizer by Amarildo that could have been cut off and losing Djalmar Santos's lob in the sun to allow Vava to score #3. It just wasn't the Cup for goalkeepers. Czechoslovakia played brilliantly in midfield, but Brazil had the experience—and in the end the game and the Cup.

1962 (Chile)

Group 1

Uruguay (0)2	**Colombia** (0)1
(Cubilla, Sasia)	(Zaluaga)
USSR (0)2	**Yugoslavia** (0)0
(Ivanov, Ponedelnik)	
Yugoslavia (2)3	**Uruguay** (1)1
(Skoblar, Galic, Jerkovic)	(Cabrera)
USSR (3)4	**Colombia** (1)4
(Ivanov 2, Chislenko, Ponedelnik)	(Aceros, Coll, Rada, Klinger)
USSR (1)2	**Uruguay** (0)1
(Mamikin, Ivanov)	(Sasia)
Yugoslavia (2)5	**Colombia** (0)0
(Galic, Jerkovic 3, Melic)	

	GP	W	D	L	GF	GA	Pts
USSR	3	2	1	0	8	5	5
Yugoslavia	3	2	0	1	8	3	4
Uruguay	3	1	0	2	4	6	2
Colombia	3	0	1	2	5	11	1

Group 2

Chile (1)3	**Switzerland** (1)1
(Sanchez, L. 2, Ramirez)	(Wuthrich)
German FR (0)0	**Italy** (0)0
Chile (0)2	**Italy** (0)0
(Ramirez, Toro)	
German FR (1)2	**Switzerland** (1)1
(Brulls, Seeler)	(Schneiter)
German FR (1)2	**Chili** (0)0
(Szymaniak*, Seeler)	
Italy (1)3	**Switzerland** (0)0
(Mora, Bulgarelli 2)	

	GP	W	D	L	GF	GA	Pts
German FR	3	2	1	0	4	1	5
Chile	3	2	0	1	5	3	4
Italy	3	1	1	1	3	2	3
Switzerland	3	0	0	3	2	8	0

Group 3

Brazil (0)2	**Mexico** (0)0
(Zagalo, Pele)	
Czech (0)1	**Spain** (0)0
(Stibranyi)	
Brazil (0)0	**Czech.** (0)0
Spain (0)1	**Mexico** (0)0
(Peiro)	
Brazil (0)2	**Spain** (1)1
(Amarildo 2)	(Adelardo)
Mexico (2)3	**Czech** (1)1
(Diaz, Del Aguila, Hernandez, H.*)	(Masek)

	GP	W	D	L	GF	GA	Pts
Brazil	3	2	1	0	4	1	5
Czechoslovakia	3	1	1	1	2	3	3
Mexico	3	1	0	2	3	4	2
Spain	3	1	0	2	2	3	2

Group 4

Argentina (1)1	**Bulgaria** (0)0
(Facundo)	
Hungary (1)2	**England** (0)1
(Tichy, Albert)	(Flowers*)
England (2)3	**Argentina** (0)1
(Flowers,* Charlton. R., Greaves)	(Sanfilippo)
Hungary (4)6	**Bulgaria** (0)1
(Albert 3, Tichy 2, Solymosi)	(Sokolov)
Argentina (0)0	**Hungary** (0)0
England (0)0	**Bulgaria** (0)0

	GP	W	D	L	GF	GA	Pts
Hungary	3	2	1	0	8	2	5
England	3	1	1	1	4	3	3
Argentina	3	1	1	1	2	3	3
Bulgaria	3	0	1	2	1	7	1

Quarterfinals

Yugoslavia (1)1	**German FR** (0)0
(Radakovic)	
Brazil (1)3	**England** (1)1
(Garrincha 2, Vava)	(Hitchens)
Chile (2)2	**USSR** (1)1
(Sanchez, L., Rojas)	(Chislenko)
Czech (1)1	**Hungary** (0)0
(Scherer)	

Semifinals

Brazil (2)4	**Chile** (1)2
(Garrincha 2, Vava 2)	(Toro, Sanchez, L.*)
Czech (0)3	**Yugoslavia** (0)1
(Kadraba, Scherer 2*)	(Jerkovic)

Third Place Game (Santiago)

Chile (0)1	**Yugoslavia** (0)0
(Rojas)	

Final (Santiago, 6/17/62)

Brazil (1)3	**Czech** (1)1
(Amarildo, Zito, Vava)	(Masopust)

Brazil: Gylmar; Santos, D., Santos, N.; Zito, Mauro, Zozimo; Garrincha, Didi, Vava, Amarildo, Zagalo

Czechoslovakia: Schroiff; Titchy, Novak, Pluskal, Popluhar, Masopust; Pospichal, Scherer, Kvasnak, Kadraba, Jelinek

Referee: Latychev (USSR)

*Penalty kick goal

The Eighth World Cup
England, 1966

sites: London, White City, Sheffield, Birmingham, Liverpool, Manchester, Middlesbrough, Sunderland

71 entrants; FIFA membership 125

format: 4 groups, each advancing 2 to quarterfinals that utilize knock-out thereafter

England had looked only so-so during past World Cup appearances. Now they were the host country, and they decided to play for keeps. In preparation for the 1966 games, England had hired Sir Alf Ramsey as National Team manager (coach), a man who looked upon the Cup as the essence of the professional game. Up till this time, England had often seemed to look upon the World Cup much as America has—a nice Olympic-like amateur contest in which principal professionals, if they were allowed to play at all by their clubs, were handled as though the Cup was but spectacle. Not Sir Alf. He was a professional, and he insisted (and received) full control. The results speak for themselves (is there a message here for the United States?).

Ramsey studied his players and came up with his system—the 4-3-3. To some fans, used to more attacking players, this system seemed fatal, but not only did his "wingless wonders" win the World Cup, but Ramsey's stolid but strong 4-3-3, has become the byword in soccer formations

throughout much of the world, providing amazing defensive strength and a strong midfield without losing much on the front line.

Brazil had won two World Cup finals in a row. What was there in England, in the 4-3-3, in the brilliance of Portugal's Eusebio to deny Pele and company their rightful supremacy now? Yet 1966 was collapse time for Brazil. Pele lasted only two matches again, this time kicked horribly in Brazil's game with Hungary. Brazil did not even make the quarterfinals. And that was only one of the many upsets and surprises (and not even the greatest) of the 1966 games. But let's get on with it.

England opened Group 1 play with a less-than-auspicious scoreless tie with Uruguay, which had played virtually their whole team on defense. Then France and Mexico tied 1-1, followed by a 2-1 Uruguayan defeat of France, a 2-0 English victory over Mexico, another tie (this one between Uruguay and Mexico), and another 2-0 English victory—this over France. Summary: four teams, six games, nine goals.

40

Bene of Hungary holds up his arms in triumph as he beat Yachin, the Soviet goalie, in second-round action during their quarterfinal match. The Soviets went on to win 2–1.

A difficult moment for any Italian soccer fan. North Korea's Pak Doo Ik scores the winning goal against Italy.

Yawn. Virtually the only excitement seemed to come from off the field, when English officials insisted that Ramsey drop the aggressive Nobby Stiles after he made a controversial foul on France's Simon. Ramsey refused. Stiles stayed.

Group 2 began with a 5–0 West German defeat of Switzerland, which exhibited the brilliance of the emerging Franz Beckenbauer. The Argentina-Spain duel, won by Argentina 2–1, was physical against the Spaniards. When Germany played Argentina for what was surely the "championship" of Group 2, Germany was oddly cautious, withdrawing Beckenbauer to such an extent that his attacking skills were no use at all. Argentina again was rough—their sweeper, Albrecht, was red carded. Germany and Argentina went through to the quarterfinals.

It was in Group 3 that the demise of Brazil took place. Brazil started out workmanlike with a 2–0 win over Bulgaria. The highlight came with a Garrincha free-kick banana-shot goal, and the low came from the rough play that Bulgaria's Jetchev performed on Pele, unrestrained by the referee. This was but an omen. Brazil's next match was against Hungary. The two teams had not met since their 1954 Battle of Berne, which was the last time Brazil had been beaten in World Cup play. Although this meeting was altogether less ill-tempered, the result was the same. Pele was unfit for play after his treatment in the Bulgarian match. Hungary's attack utilized Florian Albert playing a deep front runner (like the great Hidegkuti before him). Their two strikers, Bene and Farkas, were fast and sure. Within three minutes, Bene dribbled in from the wing and put his team ahead. Brazil equalized on a goal by Tostao on a rebound from the free kick of Lima. But Albert now took

Portugal's Eusebio heads home the second goal against Brazil, knocking the two-time Cup winners out of the tournament. Portugal went on to win 3–1.

over. He and Bene combined to set up Farkas for a mercurial break from his right-wing position and score from a volley in full stride. Beautiful. Later Meszoly scored on a penalty shot for #3, and that's how it ended.

After earlier beating Hungary by the same 3–1 score that the latter later beat Brazil, Portugal met Brazil and really nailed the coffin. Brazil, desperately trying to regroup, made nine changes, including taking out their veteran keeper Gilmar for the taller but inexperienced Manga. But it was his weak punch of Eusebio's cross that set up Simoes's header at fourteen minutes into the game to put Portugal in the lead. They were never to lose that lead. Ahead 2–0 at the half on a header from Eusebio (off the head of center forward Torres), the real coup de grace came in the second half. Pele, after sitting out the game with Hungary, was back, but now was foully kicked by Morais and limped out of the game and the tournament. It was all over for Brazil, although they came back with a goal by Rildo; but then Eusebio scored his second goal—this from a corner. Brazil was out. Hungary then beat Bulgaria to go through to the quarterfinals with Portugal.

But it was in Group 4 that the most interesting battle was fought, although play began conventionally enough with a 3–0 USSR victory over North Korean (North Korea?) and Italy's defeat of Chile 2–0. When the North Koreans drew 1–1 with Chile, a few eyebrows were raised. Italy then played the tough Soviet team, losing respectably 1–0. Then the Cinderella tale began. With the English Middlesbrough crowd cheering them on, the North Koreans met Italy in what was to be considered one of the greatest upsets in World Cup history, ranking alongside America's 1–0 defeat of England in 1950. Giving no side to the Italians, the Koreans scored on a goal by inside left Pak Doo Ik in the first half, and the Italians were never able to equalize. Italian team manager Fabbri lost his job; the team lost their respect as irate,

impassioned fans pelted them with tomatoes and eggs upon their arrival in Italy. The North Koreans, on the basis of one win, one tie, and one loss, went through with the Soviets. They had not yet peaked.

The quarterfinals provided a lot to talk about. The first game, between England and Argentina, started a controversy that isn't over even today. Argentina had already earned a bad-boy reputation for their physical style of play, but their Wembley match with England earned them the epithet "animals" from none other than Alf Ramsey. The huge, arrogant Argentinian captain Rattin was red carded by the West German referee but refused to leave, arguing for eight minutes before going. Geoffrey Hurst

English captain Bobby Moore (center, in dark jersey) holds his arm aloft, but the goal belongs to West Germany in World Cup final play. England won the hard-fought match 4–2.

England's controversial third goal is shown bouncing off the crossbar onto the line. But did it cross the line? The Soviet linesman said so, and it stood. The goal was scored by Geoffrey Hurst (not shown). This photo shows England's Roger Hunt (dark shirt) looking on as German goalie Hans Tilkowski dives.

provided a devastating header for the only score.

The second quarterfinal match, between West Germany and Uruguay, was even more disgraceful. An apparent hand ball by Schnellinger was not called, followed by a freakish goal by Germany's Haller off the deflection of Held's shot. This was enough for the bad-tempered Uruguayans, who started to play rough. Trouche and Silva were sent off for kicking or fouling Emmerich and Haller respectively. Then playing short-sided, the Uruguayans were stampeded by the Germans 4–0.

But quarterfinal #3 provided the most startling news of all when after twenty-four minutes the North Koreans led the Portuguese 3–0. The world was shell-shocked. This was the first oriental country to make the World Cup quarterfinals. Now they were knocking on the semifinal door. Incredible. But the Portuguese shook their collective heads, blew away the cobwebs, and began to play. Eusebio scored twice before halftime, once on a penalty. Then in the second half, the "Black Pearl" repeated his first-half exploits, and Augusto added a fifth goal for a 5–3 Portuguese triumph. But

Geoff Hurst achieves his hat-trick with this overtime final rifle of a goal during the Cup final against Germany. England won 4–2.

the North Koreans left their mark, one remembered to this day.

Hungary and the USSR played soporifically to a 2–1 victory for the Soviets on two mistakes from the Hungarian goalie Gelei, who fumbled a shot and then failed to hold a cross (meanwhile, Rakosi missed a simple shot).

The German-Soviet semifinal was less than awe-inspiring, with Chislenko sent off for injuring Held after himself being kicked by Schnellinger. Meanwhile Szabo was hurt but limped about the field, and the Germans had

to struggle against nine fit men to eke out a 2–1 victory.

The other semifinal—between England and Portugal—was a fine one. England finally showed some brilliance in attack, as though they possessed something more than Sir Alf's famous system and the British crowds. Bobby Charlton scored twice for England—the first coming before the half after Portugal's keeper Pereira managed only to deflect Hunt's shot and #2 coming in the second half off a pass from Hurst, who was the hero in the final. Nobby Stiles stuck to the brilliant Eusebio like a close member of the family. Portugal's only score was on a penalty shot by Eusebio (this was the first score against England in the tournament). England went through 2–1 and Portugal beat the Soviets 2–1 (the three preceding games—the two semifinals and the last quarterfinal match—were all by a similar score) for third place (again, Eusebio scored from the penalty spot).

The final was a beauty. Germany withdrew Beckenbauer to cover Bobby Charlton. A mistake. Even so, they scored first on a shot by Haller off the head of English fullback Wilson. Within six minutes Geoff Hurst equalized from West Ham clubmate Bobby Moore's free kick. Then, in the second half, the other West Ham player, Martin Peters, sent a beautiful volley into the nets. Now the Cup was within sight, and Alf Ramsey's early prediction ("We will win the Cup") seemed to be coming true. But in the last minute of play (yes, the last minute), Jack Charlton fouled Held, and the free kick by Emmerich rebounded to Weber who inched the ball in along the far post. Tied at the whistle—and into extra time.

A beautiful pass from Alan Ball to Geoff Hurst set up one of the most controversial goals in World Cup history (and certainly the most controversial in a final) when the shot bounded off the crossbar down on the goal line. Hunt, who was poised to make the final touch, turned away with his arms raised in victory. But was it a goal? The Germans thought the ball had not crossed the line, but the Soviet linesman disagreed, and the goal counted. Still debated in many pubs, the third goal was the subject of a book all its own, with many pictures. In the future, FIFA must give great

consideration to introducing different electronic devices that could eliminate such difficult decisions. The controversy surrounding the third goal is still unsettled, but what finally was settled that day was accomplished again by Geoff Hurst off a pass from Moore—a splendid left-footed rifle into the nets for the first World Cup final hat-trick. England had won.

1966 (England)

Group 1

England	(0)0	Uruguay	(0)0
France	(0)1	Mexico	(0)1
(Hausser)		(Borja)	
Uruguay	(2)2	France	(1)1
(Rocha, Cortex)		De Bourgoing*	
England	(1)2	Mexico	(0)0
(Charlton, R., Hunt)			
Uruguay	(0)0	Uruguay	(0)0
England	(1)2	France	(0)0
(Hunt 2)			

	GP	W	D	L	GF	GA	Pts
England	3	2	1	0	4	0	5
Uruguay	3	1	2	0	2	1	4
Mexico	3	0	2	1	1	3	2
France	3	0	1	2	2	5	1

Group 2

German FR	(3)5	Switzerland	(0)0
(Held, Haller 2*,			
Beckenbauer 2)			
Argentina	(0)2	Spain	(0)1
(Artime 2)		(Pirri)	
Spain	(0)2	Switzerland	(1)1
(Sanchis, Amancio)		(Quentin)	
Argentina	(0)0	German FR	(0)0
Argentina	(0)2	Switzerland	(0)0
(Artime, Onega)			
German FR	(1)2	Spain	(1)1
(Emmerich, Seeler)		(Fuste)	

	GP	W	D	L	GF	GA	Pts
German FR	3	2	1	0	7	1	5
Argentina	3	2	1	0	4	1	5
Spain	3	1	0	2	4	5	2
Switzerland	3	0	0	3	1	9	0

Group 3

Brazil	(1)2	Bulgaria	(0)0
(Pele, Garrincha)			
Portugal	(1)3	Hungary	(0)1
(Augusto 2, Torres)		(Bene)	
Hungary	(1)3	Brazil	(1)1
(Bene, Farkas,		(Tostao)	
Meszoly*)			
Portugal	(2)3	Bulgaria	(0)0
(Vutzov, o.g.,			
Eusebio, Torres)			
Portugal	(2)3	Brazil	(0)1
(Simoes, Eusebio 2)		(Rildo)	
Hungary	(2)3	Bulgaria	(1)1
(Davidov, o.g.,		(Asparoukhov)	
Meszoly, Bene)			

	GP	W	D	L	GF	GA	Pts
Portugal	3	3	0	0	9	2	6
Hungary	3	2	0	1	7	5	4
Brazil	3	1	0	2	4	6	2
Bulgaria	3	0	0	3	1	8	0

Group 4

USSR	(2)3	Korea DPR	(0)0
(Malafeev 2,			
Banischevsky)			
Italy	(1)2	Chile	(0)0
(Mazzola, Barison)			
Chile	(1)1	Korea DPR	(0)1
(Marcos*)		(Pak Seung Jin)	
USSR	(0)1	Italy	(0)0
(Chislenko)			
Korea DPR	(1)1	Italy	(0)0
(Pak Doo Ik)			
USSR	(1)2	Chile	(1)1
(Porkujan 2)		(Marcos)	

	GP	W	D	L	GF	GA	Pts
USSR	3	3	0	0	6	1	6
Korea DPR	3	1	1	1	2	4	3
Italy	3	1	0	2	2	2	2
Chile	3	0	1	2	2	5	1

Quarterfinals

England	(0)1	Argentina	(0)0
(Hurst)			
German FR	(1)4	Uruguay	(0)0
(Held, Beckenbauer,			
Seeler, Haller)			
Portugal	(2)5	Korea DPR	(3)3
(Eusenbio 4**,		(Pak Seung Jin,	
Augusto)		Yang Sung Kook,	
		Li Dong Woon)	
USSR	(1)2	Hungary	(0)1
(Chislenko, Porku-		(Bene)	
jan)			

Semifinals

German FR	(1)2	USSR	(0)1
(Haller, Beckenbauer)		(Porkujan)	
England	(1)2	Portugal	(0)1
(Charlton, R. 2)		(Eusebio*)	

Third Place Game (London)

| Portugal | (1)2 | USSR | (1)1 |
| (Eusebio*, Torres) | | (Malafeev) | |

Final (London, 7/30/66)

| England | (1)(2)4 | German FR | (1)(2)2 |
| (Hurst 3, Peters) | | (Haller, Weber) | |

England: Banks; Cohen, Wilson; Stiles, Charlton, J., Moore; Ball, Hurst, Hunt, Charlton R., Peters

German FR: Tilkowski; Hottges, Schnellinger; Beckenbauer, Schulz, Weber; Held, Haller, Seeler, Overath, Emmerich

Referee: Dienst (Switzerland)

The Ninth World Cup
Mexico, 1970

sites: Mexico City, Puebla, Toluca, Guadalajara, Leon
73 entrants; FIFA membership 138

format: 4 groups, each advancing 2 to quarterfinals that utilize knock-out thereafter

With the remarkable showing of the North Koreans in the 1966 World Cup, more and more Third World countries sought advancement in Cup play. In 1970, Morocco and Israel were among the sixteen finalists, and in the future other emerging countries would play (Zaire in 1974, Iran and Tunisia in 1978, and the Cameroon, Kuwait, and Algeria in 1982).

With perhaps England and Brazil the cofavorites, there were still many unanswered questions about several teams. The strong West Germans had in Beckenbauer and Gerd Müller a wonderful combination. Could Italy, newly crowned European champs, erase the stain on their reputation accomplished four years earlier? Could the heralded Peruvians, managed by Didi of Brazil, live up to their pre-Cup publicity?

But after Mexico was awarded the games (the first and so far the only CONCACAF nation to host the World Cup), the greatest question mark of all concerned the altitude and heat of that Central American country. Although the climate of Mexico was more akin to South America than it was to Europe, no other country practiced daily at altitudes of 7,800 feet above sea level. To make matters more intolerable, games would be played in the full heat of the day to accommodate TV coverage to Europe. This would be an exhausting World Cup for all concerned.

Group 1 proved that it would be

Pele jumps in triumph after scoring one of his two goals against Romania in first-round play. Brazil won 3–2.

Brazil's Jairzinho shows his jubilation as he nails the coffin of Peru in quarterfinal play in Mexico City. Brazil won 4–2 . . . on their way to the Cup championship.

exhausting for the spectators as well, as Mexico and the USSR squared off to a scoreless tie, made more demanding by the innumerable penalties called. And even though the combined six games in Group 1 produced fifteen goals—two and one-half times as many as were made in Group 2!—only one losing team managed to compile even one goal, that being Belgium in its 4–1 loss to the Soviets (this was before Belgian players, falling out with one another over which shoe to wear, made a show of disunity; the Czechs went even further in their capitalistic arguments, being suspended for it in the process). Otherwise, the scores were shut-outs, everyone picking on poor El Salvador (Belgium by 3–0, Mexico 4–0, and the Soviets 2–0). And to think that El

Salvador's qualification in CONCACAF over bitter rival Honduras led to the Soccer War that eventually cost 3,000 lives and has caused ill will to this day! A country that takes losing that seriously should have been able to score a goal. After drawing with the Soviets, Mexico lucked out. One of their four goals against hapless El Salvador was on a free kick awarded to El Salvador but taken by Mexico. Their squeaky 1–0 victory over Belgium resulted from a very doubtful penalty. But it was enough, as Mexico joined the Soviets through to the quarterfinals.

But the heat seemed to be the principal victor in Group 2. A total of six(!) goals were produced for the six games played. Were it not for the

Top photo shows Jairzinho and Italy's Giacinto Facchetti during the World Cup final, which Brazil won, 4–1. Other photo shows an Italian defender's tackle of Rivelino during the final.

rhubarb caused by the dropping of Gianni Rivera in favor of Sandro Mazzola (eventually compromised by having Mazzola play the first half and Rivera the second), there would have been nothing to stave off the sandman. This compromise was possible because

1970 marked the first time substitutes could be used in World Cup competition. Italy retained the best record in Group 2 on the basis of one win and two draws. They had produced a grand total of one goal in group play. Uruguay, with a win, a loss, and a tie, joined them (they had two goals).

At least one couldn't hear the snoring during Group 3 games. In fact, one could hardly hear anything. You see, the English had come to town with a bad-boy image, made implausibly stronger by the arrest in Bogota of English captain Bobby Moore on the trumped-up charge of stealing a diamond bracelet (this ludicrous charge was not cleared up for years, but it placed a stain on the English reputation in Mexico). Sir Alf Ramsey does not suffer fools gladly, and he was less than compassionate to Mexican journalists who invaded his practice fields, ignoring his schedules. The result was that the Union Jack was booed at the opening ceremony, and the English team had to put up with a constant cacophany from upbraided Mexicans wherever they went—even to the point of serenading them outside their hotel with chants, hoots, and car horns throughout the night—all undisturbed by the local gendarmes, of course. Not the kind of stuff that cements good relations.

The Romanians, however, made sure the English players wouldn't fall asleep, brutalizing them before the benevolent eyes of the Belgian referee—Romanian left fullback Mocanu kicking at least two English players. But England won 1–0. Then Czechoslovakia scored first on the favored Brazilians, but with Pele and Jairzinho in top form, Brazil could not be denied. The result was a 4–1 win and the set up for what many had thought would be the dress rehearsal for the final—Brazil v. England. It was nearly 100 degrees outside as a weary English team took the field against the most talented side in the tournament (perhaps any World Cup tournament). The first half witnessed one of the greatest saves in World Cup history when Pele headed a Jairzinho cross down to avoid the keeper's dive. But

Jairzinho right after he scored goal no. 3 for Brazil during the Cup final. Facchetti, the Italian captain, is at left, and Italy's keeper, Enrico Albertosi, lies on the ground.

Gordon Banks somehow managed to twist backwards and up to scoop the ball over the bar. The astounded Pele could do nothing but applaud the unbelievable save. Later, after England had missed two great chances, Tostao crossed the ball in from the left, Pele through passed to Jairzinho, who scored. Two more chances for England, one coming on an open goal, led to the 1–0 defeat. But England later defeated the Czechs on a penalty shot awarded dubiously and went through with Brazil to the quarterfinals.

The shock in Group 4 came from seeing Germany trail Morocco until late in their game when two quick goals from Seeler and Müller saved the day. Peru, in the meantime, had showed its mettle by defeating Bulgaria 3–2 after being down 2–0, then took care of Morocco 3–0. But the Germans recovered their form after their game with Morocco and beat Bulgaria 5–2 on Müller's hat trick, then took care of Peru 3–1, although the South American team still went through.

As is so often the case, the quarterfinals were better than group play. In Mexico City, the sole score in Uruguay's extra-time win over the USSR was a controversial one, since it seemed certain that the ball had gone out of play before Cubilla's cross to the scorer Esparrago. Italy, tied 1–1 with Mexico at half, must have read their own pre-Cup billing, pulled themselves together and took Mexico apart 4–1. Then Tostao scored twice and Rivelino and Jairzinho (who scored in every game for Brazil) once as Brazil defeated the game Peruvians 4–2.

But the best game by far was the West German-English match in Leon.

The great Banks was ill and missed the game. His replacement, Peter Bonetti, had not played for a month; he caused at least one, if not all three, German goals. But the beginning was all England, with a first-half goal by Mullery, followed by a second-half score from Peters, making it 2–0, England. But then Ramsey, apparently fearful of the intense heat and perhaps thinking the game had been won, made one of those tactical decisions that become the favorite conversation of second-guessing fans for years and years. He took out both Peters and Bobby Charlton, and the Germans put in speedy winger Grabowski. Beckenbauer then sent a shot that bounced under Bonetti's body, and Seeler later followed up with a tremendous back-header to equalize and send the game into extra time. This set up the final comeback goal by Müller for the German win.

The Germans were exhausted from their extra-time match with England when they took the field against the Italians, who had had it easy with Mexico. Behind by a goal at the half, the Germans equalized in the second period to send the game into extra time. So far it had been ninety minutes and two goals. But during the next half hour (two fifteen-minute overtime periods) five more goals went up on the scoreboard—two for the Germans and three for the Italians. Beckenbauer injured his shoulder and played the rest of the game taped up. Germany's goal-making machine Gerd Müller scored two in a losing effort.

In Guadalajara, Uruguay struck first, bouncing a ball past the vulnerable Brazilian goalie Felix. But quite frankly goalkeeping (in fact, even defense) wasn't really what this Brazilian team was all about. To beat them you had to outscore them, and that was not easy. Clodoaldo equalized late in the first half. Jairzinho scored with fourteen minutes remaining, and Rivelino's last-minute score certified it for Brazil. West Germany later beat Uruguay 1–0 for third place.

Brazil opened scoring in the final on a header; then Italy equalized just before half. After that, it was all Brazil. A fine left-foot shot outside the box by Gerson was #2, followed up by an indirect touched by Pele, kicked by Gerson, and scored by Jairzinho, and finally captain Carlos Alberto scored the fourth. It was the first time since 1958 that Pele finished a World Cup uninjured. It was to be his last. And what a finale. On the basis of winning the Cup three times, Brazil was awarded the Jules Rimet World Cup trophy permanently. There would have to be a new trophy for 1974.

1970 (Mexico)

Group 1

Mexico	(0)0	USSR	(0)0
Belgium	(1)3	El Salvador	(0)0
(Van Moer 2, Lambert*)			
USSR	(1)4	Belgium	(0)1
(Byshovets 2, Asatiani, Khmelnitsky)		(Lambert)	
Mexico	(1)4	El Salvador	(0)0
(Valdivia 2, Fragoso, Basaguren)			
USSR	(0)2	El Salvador	(0)0
(Byshovets 2)			
Mexico	(1)1	Belgium	(0)0
(Pena*)			

	GP	W	D	L	GF	GA	Pts
USSR	3	2	1	0	6	1	5
Mexico	3	2	1	0	5	0	5
Belgium	3	1	0	2	4	5	2
El Salvador	3	0	0	3	0	9	0

Group 2

Uruguay	(1)2	Israel	(0)0
(Maneiro, Mujica)			
Italy	(1)1	Sweden	(0)0
(Domenghini)			
Uruguay	(0)0	Italy	(0)0
Sweden	(0)1	Israel	(0)1
(Turesson)		(Spiegler)	
Sweden	(0)1	Uruguay	(0)0
(Grahn)			
Italy	(0)0	Israel	(0)0

	GP	W	D	L	GF	GA	Pts
Italy	3	1	2	0	1	0	4
Uruguay	3	1	1	1	2	1	3
Sweden	3	1	1	1	2	2	3
Israel	3	0	2	1	1	3	2

Group 3

England	(0)1	Romania	(0)0
(Hurst)			
Brazil	(1)4	Czech	(1)1
(Rivelino, Pele, Jairzinho 2)		(Petras)	
Romania	(0)2	Czech	(1)1
(Neagu, Dumitrache)		(Petras)	
Brazil	(0)1	England	(0)0
(Jairzinho)			
Brazil	(2)3	Romania	(0)2
(Pele 2, Jairzinho)		(Dumitrache, Dembrovski)	
England	(0)1	Czech	(0)0
(Clarke*)			

	GP	W	D	L	GF	GA	Pts
Brazil	3	3	0	0	8	3	6
England	3	2	0	1	2	1	4
Romania	3	1	0	2	4	5	2
Czechoslovakia	3	0	0	3	2	7	0

Group 4

Peru	(0)3	Bulgaria	(1)2
(Gallardo, Chumpitaz, Cubillas)		(Dermendjiev, Bonev)	
German FR	(0)2	Morocco	(1)1
(Seeler, Muller)		(Houmane)	
Peru	(0)3	Morocco	(0)0
(Cubillas 2, Challe)			
German FR	(2)5	Bulgaria	(1)2
(Libuda, Muller 3, Seeler)		(Nikodimov, Kolev)	
German FR	(3)3	Peru	(1)1
(Muller 3)		(Cubillas)	
Bulgaria	(1)1	Morocco	(0)1
(Jetchev)		(Ghazouani)	

	GP	W	D	L	GF	GA	Pts
German FR	3	3	0	0	10	4	6
Peru	3	2	0	1	7	5	4
Bulgaria	3	0	1	2	5	9	1
Morocco	3	0	1	2	2	6	1

QUARTERFINALS

Uruguay	(0)(0)1	USSR	(0)(0)0
(Esparrago)			
Italy	(1)4	Mexico	(1)1
(Domenghini, Riva 2, Rivera)		(Gonzales)	
Brazil	(2)4	Peru	(1)2
(Rivelino, Tostao 2, Jairzinho)		Gallardo, Cubillas	

German FR	(0)(2)3	England	(1)(2)2
(Beckenbauer, Seeler, Muller)		(Mullery, Peters)	

QUARTERFINALS

Uruguay	(0)(0)1	USSR	(0)(0)0
(Esparrago)			
Italy	(1)4	Mexico	(1)1
(Domenghini, Riva 2, Rivera)		(Gonzales)	
Brazil	(2)4	Peru	(1)2
(Rivelino, Tostao 2, Jairzinho)		(Gallardo, Cubillas)	
German FR	(0)(2)3	England	(1)(2)2
(Beckenbauer, Seeler, Muller)		(Mullery, Peters)	

SEMIFINALS

Italy	(1)(1)4	German FR	(0)(1)3
(Boninsegna, Burgnich, Riva, Rivera)		(Schnellinger, Muller 2)	
Brazil	(1)3	Uruguay	(1)1
(Clodoaldo, Jairzinho, Rivelino)		(Cubilla)	

THIRD PLACE GAME (Mexico City)

German FR	(1)1	Uruguay	(0)0
(Overath)			

FINAL (Mexico City, 6/20/70)

Brazil	(1)4	Italy	(1)1
(Pele, Gerson, Jairzinho, Carlos Alberto)		(Boninsegna)	

Brazil: Feliz; Carlos Alberto, Brito, Wilson, Piazza, Everaldo; Clodoaldo, Gerson; Jairzinho, Tostao, Pele, Rivelino

Italy: Albertosi; Burgnich, Cera, Rosato, Facchetti; Bertini (s. Juliano), Mazzola, De Sisti; Domenghini, Boninsegna (s. Rivera), Riva

Referee: Glockner (East Germany)

The Tenth World Cup
West Germany, 1974

sites: Dusseldorf, Munich, Stuttgart
95 entrants; FIFA membership 140

format: 4 groups, each advancing 2 to 2 further groups, which play round robin (cup) to determine 2 winners to play for the finals and 2 second-place finishers to play for third place

The 1974 World Cup was the best organized and executed of any before or since. West Germany was host, and they were the model of efficiency both on and off the field. The stadia were immaculate, and the playing surfaces superb. Germany had the energy, know-how, and team to be the best (West Germany had bested the Soviets 3–0 in 1972 for the European Championship). Moreover, the qualifying sixteen were better prepared than ever before. This was destined to be a great Cup race.

Holland's Johnny Rep raises his hands and Johann Cruyff shows his happiness upon scoring the second and final goal in Holland's shutout of Brazil.

Germany had built its team around the bloc of Bayern Munich players (Beckenbauer, Müller, Maier, Breitner, Schwarzerbeck, and Hoeness). The World Cup final would be played in Bayern's Olympic Stadium.

It seemed that Germany's main competition would be European. The South American teams were less threatening now, with some of their big guns (Pele most of all) gone. Gone too was the English team, which did not make the final sixteen for the first time since 1950. The Soviets eliminated themselves because after winning a qualifying group they were required to play against the winners of South

Above: Poland's Lato (right) is congratulated by teammate Deyna after Lato scored what proved to be the only goal of the game against Brazil to decide the third-place winner. Below: the controversial play in the opening moments of the finals, as Johann Cruyff is taken down in the penalty area. Neeskens scored the penalty shot, but that was all the scoring for Holland, as West Germany won 2–1.

Three of the great stars of the 1974 World Cup: Johann Cruyff (no. 14) looks on as the West German goalie Sepp Maier writhes in agony and Franz Beckenbauer (no. 5) raises his hand for time.

American Group 3, which happened to be Chile. For political reasons, the Soviets refused to play in Santiago, so FIFA awarded a berth to Chile. Among the strong European teams to be reckoned with were Poland, East Germany, and Yugoslavia.

But it was the Netherlands that provided the most competition. Like tiny Hungary in the mid-fifties, Holland in the mid-seventies was definitely the most skilled and exciting team in the world. Built around their fabulous ball-control expert Johann Cruyff, a player of such deft touch and incredible explosive power that he can

only be compared to Pele. Like Germany, Holland had built its team around a bloc of players, but from two teams, Ajax and Feyenoord (even their manager, Rinus Michels, came from Ajax—he was the one who had built them for their three consecutive European Cup triumphs in 1971, 1972, and 1973). The attacking talent alongside the incomparable Cruyff included Johan Neeskens, Johnny Rep, Wim Van Hanegem, and Rob Resenbrink.

The Dutch brand of soccer had dominated Western Europe for several years. They built their entire system

Left: action during the World Cup final, won by West Germany 2–1. The photo shows Holland's Rene Van Der Kerkhof (darker uniform) with an unidentified German player. Below: Gerd Müller, who scored the only nonpenalty shot of the final, rifles the ball directly into the raised hands of Holland's Jongbloed. Müller's goal came with but two minutes remaining in the half, but it proved to be the last goal of the day. Earlier Neeskens (Holland) and Breitner (Germany) scored from the penalty spot.

around Cruyff, playing an amazingly free-flowing, lightning-quick style—*total soccer*. Moving away from positional understanding to what one could call "reactive interpositions" in which players would take other positions during the quick buildup toward the goal. Holding back virtually nothing on attack, their arrogance and style seemed unbeatable. The plan was always to find Cruyff and while he was in possession of the ball, the other players would run into attacks without fear, interchanging positions and creating space for each other by the exchange. Exciting soccer.

With unknowns Haiti and Zaire providing very little (but with Australia gallant in defeat), the main curiosity of the opening rounds seemed to be the draw that placed both East and West Germany in Group 1. After the 1972 Munich Olympics tragedy, the West Germans wanted nothing of the kind of terrorism that marked those games. They beefed up security to take on any contingency.

In Group 1's opener, West Germany didn't exactly make mincemeat of Chile, beating them 1–0, while their brethren to the east were equally unimpressive against Australia, 2–0 (taking nearly an hour to score—and that by Australia's Curran's deflection that went into his own net). Australia looked good against the West Germans too, missing a couple of close shots before Germany scored twice to win. East Germany drew with Chile, which did the same against Australia, setting up the finale for Group 1—West v. East Germany.

The East Germans kept eight field players in defensive positions, gambling

everything on a breakaway—which paid off in the second half, but it took some luck to keep the West Germans down, Grabowski missing a great opportunity and Müller hitting the post. Both Germanies went through to the second tier.

Group 2 provided the odd result of having only three of the six games resulting in wins—all of them losses by Zaire. The rest were ties, so there would have to be one unbeaten team that did not go through to the second tier. And that team was Scotland, having defeated Zaire by a mere 2–0, whereas cautious Brazil had won 3–0 and Yugoslavia 9–0. Yugoslavia should have been able to beat Brazil in the opener, either by several shots that just missed or hit the post or by a penalty shot that should have been called, but was not, when Acimovic was taken down by two defenders. It didn't help Scotland that they had outplayed both Yugoslavia and Brazil in its matches with them—the scores still stood tied, and the advancement in this Cup would be by goal difference (not average). (After Scotland's draw with Brazil, boisterous Scottish fans almost took the city of Frankfurt apart. It took a strong warning from the German government to tame them.) So Scotland, undefeated, was eliminated.

Holland began Group 3 brilliantly against Uruguay 2–0 on two goals by Johnny Rep, followed by a scoreless tie with Sweden, and a 4–1 trouncing of Bulgaria. Sweden, which drew with Bulgaria and beat Uruguay, accompanied the Dutch to the next tier of play.

Group 4 provided the best competition. Except for weak-sister

Haiti, Group 4 had three strong teams in Italy, Argentina, and Poland. Italy had put together a string of impressive internationals without allowing a score until Haiti's one known player, Emmanuel Sanon, scored in the second half. It was the first time in thirteen internationals (in 1,143 minutes of soccer) that a goal had been scored against the Italians. But it was not enough, as Italy scored three to beat Haiti 3–1.

The 3–2 Polish defeat of Argentina was an impressive affair, both teams sparkling but Argentina providing costly defensive mistakes. Then Italy provided Argentina with an own goal, tying them in the process 1–1, while Poland unraveled Haiti 7–0. Argentina later beat Haiti 4–1, and Poland beat the demoralized Italians 2–1. Argentina, having scored seven goals and given up five, went through on goal difference, since the Italians had scored five and given up four. Italy departed vowing to become a more offense-minded team than catenaccio, a basically defensive orientation, allowed them to be.

Now the eight qualifiers were arranged in two further groups for cup play. Group A consisted of the Netherlands, Brazil, East Germany, and Argentina; Group B had Poland, West Germany, Sweden, and Yugoslavia.

The Dutch seemed to grow stronger as the tournament progressed, shutting out Argentina (4–0), East Germany (2–0), and Brazil (2–0) to go through to the final. After crippling Argentina, Holland took on the East Germans, who wisely covered Cruyff man-to-man. But that didn't prevent two sure goals by Rensenbrink and Neeskens.

Brazil had earlier blanked East Germany 1–0, then defeated Argentina 2–1 (the Brazilians' first goal of the tournament). But this was not the same Brazil that had won three World Cups. They fought the Dutch with violence rather than skill, and Luis Pereira was red carded. Two tremendous goals, first by Neeskens and then by Cruyff, sent the Netherlands through to the final. Cruyff's goal is worthy of additional comment, since it was one of the truly great scores in World Cup competition. Cruyff served a penetrating pass to the left, then ran twenty yards at full speed into the penalty box to receive the ball in the air at the ten-yard line. Without breaking stride, he hammered the ball into the back of the net with the inside of his right foot on one touch. Absolutely thrilling.

Group B shaped up to be a West German-Polish affair. Both sides had grown impressively stronger as the competition continued, and both took turns beating Sweden and Yugoslavia by relatively close scores (one or two goals) until their meeting as Group B's finale. But the real star seemed to be the weather. Frankfurt was pounded with a downpour an hour or so before the game, and the game was held up while the fire department pumped off thousands of gallons of water from the pitch. Poland, which relied heavily on quick counters to front runners Lato (the scoring champion of the Cup), Gadocha, and Szarmach, simply could not play that kind of game on this kind of field. Germany, on the other hand, had wanted to attack carefully, using Beckenbauer's impressive abilities to build up and free Müller. Puddles of water and mud got in their way too. Beckenbauer quickly figured out how to play in the water, scooping the ball out of the water instead of making ground passes. The keepers began to send long kicks into the air, hoping to capitalize on their opponents' defensive mistakes. So the game became a kicking contest for goalkeepers. Midfield play was eliminated. Poland relied on pushing the ball wide to the green, playable turf. Germany played more up the middle, naturally, to free Müller and Hoeness. This was much more difficult, since most of the mud was in the center of the field.

Poland looked strong in the first half, and Maier had to be extremely sharp to prevent a Gadocha free kick and a breakaway of Lato from becoming goals. In the second half, Zmuda fouled Holzenbein on a slide tackle, and a penalty shot was given. But the incredible Polish goalie Tamaszewski saved the Hoeness kick, and the game remained scoreless. Eventually, Holzenbein opened to Müller for the game's only goal. Poland went on to beat Brazil 1–0 for third place.

So it was to be the pretourney favorites, the Netherlands and West Germany, playing for the World Cup. Germany was playing at home (indeed, the home of its bloc team Bayern Munich), but Holland's own bloc team, Ajax, had demolished Bayern Munich prior to the Cup. Would the psychological edge belong to Holland?

Certainly no final began with such excitement. The Dutch kicked off and played a series of fifteen unbroken passes up to and across the face of Germany's penalty area. Suddenly,

Cruyff exploded into the penalty area and was brought down by Hoeness. Penalty shot. Neeskens put it through. With ninety seconds gone, it was the Netherlands 1, West Germany 0. But after the first ten minutes, it seemed as though the Dutch players became complacent. Their intensity began to disappear. Berti Vogts of Germany was the marker assigned to cover Cruyff. Vogts, considered one of the best defenders in the world, was to pick up the flying Dutchman when he arrived in the defensive third of the field. But under these conditions, Vogts would have Cruyff coming at him at full speed. It would be difficult to strip the ball from such as Cruyff in this way, being flat-footed against the world's greatest attacker. So, after receiving a yellow card, Vogts went to his Coach Schoen and suggested that he pick up Cruyff all over the field. Schoen agreed, and Vogts put on a great show, shadowing Cruyff wherever he went, often stripping him of the ball—one time going into the goal mouth and volleying the bouncing ball over the crossbar. Cruyff could not play his game and became frustrated. The Dutch players held back and no longer ran with reckless abandon toward the goal.

In the twenty-sixth minute, the Germans counterattacked on the left, and Holzenbein dribbled into the penalty area and was cut down by Jansen. This time it was Paul Breitner's penalty kick that tied the score.

Cruyff surged forward, going deep to collect passes — only to be shadowed by Vogts. Finally, another great German counterattack, this time from the right. Bonhof beat Haan and crossed to Müller, who almost misfired. On his second attempt, however, he squeezed the ball past Jongbloed to go ahead 2–1, and that's how it was at the half.

In the second half, the Dutch came out smoking. But the stubborn German defense, led by Vogts, Maier, and Beckenbauer, stood firm, Maier particularly was spectacular, once taking a full volley from Rep at the six yard line and blocking it with his body. On this day, he was unbeatable.

Holland dominated the second half, giving the Germans all they could handle. Breitner and Bonhof cleared the German line, and Maier was unwavering in goal. Heroics all around in this final. But though they dominated, the Dutch couldn't score again, and at the whistle the wreath belonged to Germany.

With a foundation set by Sepp Herberger and his direct descendant, Helmut Schoen, the Germans had again taken on the best in the world and prevailed.

1974 (West Germany)

GROUP 1

German FR (1)1		Chile	(0)0
(Breitner)			
German DR (0)2		Australia	(0)0
(Curran, o.g., Streich)			
German FR (2)3		Australia	(0)0
(Overath, Cullmann, Müller)			
Chile (0)1		German DR	(0)1
(Ahumada)		(Hoffman)	
Australia (0)0		Chile	(0)0
German DR (0)1		German FR	(0)0
(Sparwasser)			

	GP	W	D	L	GF	GA	Pts
German DR	3	2	1	0	4	1	5
German FR	3	2	0	1	4	1	4
Chile	3	0	2	1	1	2	2
Australia	3	0	1	2	0	5	1

GROUP 2

Brazil (0)0		Yugoslavia	(0)0
Scotland (2)2		Zaire	(0)0
(Lorimar, Jordan)			
Yugoslavia (6)9		Zaire	(0)0
(Bajevic 3, Dzajic, Surjek, Katalinski, Bogicevic, Oblak, Petkovic)			
Scotland (0)0		Brazil	(0)0
Brazil (1)3		Zaire	(0)0
(Jairzinho, Rivelino, Valdomiro)			
Scotland (0)1		Yugoslavia	(0)1
(Jordan)		(Karasic)	

	GP	W	D	L	GF	GA	Pts
Yugoslavia	3	1	2	0	10	1	4
Brazil	3	1	2	0	3	0	4
Scotland	3	1	2	0	3	1	4
Zaire	3	0	0	3	0	14	0

GROUP 3

Sweden (0)0		Bulgaria	(0)0
Netherlands (1)2		Uruguay	(0)0
(Rep 2)			
Netherlands (0)0		Sweden	(0)0
Bulgaria (0)1		Uruguay	(0)1
(Bonev)		(Pavoni)	
Sweden (0)3		Uruguay	(0)0
(Edstroem 2, Sandberg)			
Netherlands (2)4		Bulgaria	(0)1
(Neeskens 2**, Rep, de Jong)		(Krol, o.g.)	

	GP	W	D	L	GF	GA	Pts
Netherlands	3	2	1	0	6	1	5
Sweden	3	1	2	0	3	0	4
Bulgaria	3	0	2	1	2	5	2
Uruguay	3	0	1	2	1	6	1

GROUP 4

Italy (0)3		Haiti	(0)1
(Rivera, Benetti, Anastasi)		(Sanon)	
Poland (2)3		Argentina	(0)2
(Lato 2, Szarmach)		(Heredia, Babington)	
Poland (5)7		Haiti	(0)0
(Lato 2, Deyna, Szarmach 3, Gorgon)			
Argentina (1)1		Italy	(1)1
(Houseman)		(Perfumo, o.g.)	
Argentina (2)4		Haiti	(0)1
(Yazalde 2, Houseman, Ayala)		(Sanon)	
Poland (2)2		Italy	(0)1
(Szarmach, Deyna)		(Capello)	

	GP	W	D	L	GF	GA	Pts
Poland	3	3	0	0	12	3	6
Argentina	3	1	1	1	7	5	3
Italy	3	1	1	1	5	4	3
Haiti	3	0	0	3	2	14	0

SECOND ROUND

GROUP A

Netherlands (2)4		Argentina	(0)0
(Cruyff 2, Rep, Krol)			
Brazil (0)1		German DR	(0)0
(Rivelino)			
Netherlands (1)2		German DR	(0)0
(Neeskens, Resenbrink)			
Brazil (1)2		Argentina	(1)1
(Rivelino, Jairzinho)		(Brindisi)	
Netherlands (0)2		Brazil	(0)0
(Neeskens, Cruyff)			
Argentina (1)1		German DR	(1)1
(Houseman)		(Streich)	

	GP	W	D	L	GF	GA	Pts
Netherlands	3	3	0	0	8	0	6
Brazil	3	2	0	1	3	3	4
German DR	3	0	1	2	1	4	1
Argentina	3	0	1	2	2	7	1

GROUP B

German FR (0)2		Yugoslavia	(0)0
(Breitner, Müller)			
Poland (1)1		Sweden	(0)0
(Lato)			
Poland (1)2		Yugoslavia	(1)1
(Denya*, Lato)		(Karasi)	
German FR (0)4		Sweden	(1)2
(Overath, Bonhof, Grabowski, Hoeness*)		(Edstroem, Sandberg)	
German FR (0)1		Poland	(0)0
(Müller)			
Sweden (1)2		Yugoslavia	(1)1
(Edstroem, Torstensson)		(Surjek)	

	GP	W	D	L	GF	GA	Pts
German FR	3	3	0	0	7	2	6
Poland	3	2	0	1	3	2	4
Sweden	3	1	0	2	4	6	2
Yugoslavia	3	0	0	3	2	6	0

THIRD PLACE GAME (Munich)

Poland (0)1		Brazil	(0)0
(Lato)			

FINAL (Munich, 7/7/74)

German FR (2)2		Netherlands	(1)1
(Breitner*, Müller)		(Neeskens*)	

German FR: Maier; Vogts, Beckenbauer, Schwarzenbeck, Breitner; Hoeness, Bonhof, Overath; Grabowski, Müller, Holzenbein

Netherlands: Jongbloed; Suurbier, Rijsbergen (s. de Jong), Haan, Krol; Jansen, Neeskens, van Hanagem; Rep, Cruyff, Resenbrink (s. R. van der Kerkhof)

Referee: Taylor (England)

*Penalty goal kick

The Eleventh World Cup
Argentina, 1978

sites: Buenos Aires, Mar del Plata, Rusario, Cordoba, Mendoza
105 entrants; FIFA membership 146

format: 4 groups each advancing 2 to 2 further groups, which play round robin to determine 2 winners to play for finals and 2 second-place finishers to play for third place

The June 25, 1978, World Cup final was viewed by 1 billion people—the largest ever to watch a single sporting event. Soccer was the lifeblood of whole nations now. Virtually the entire world belonged to FIFA (its 146 members surpassed the membership in the United Nations).

Argentina worked hard, refurbishing old stadia and building several new ones, to satisfy the anticipated crowds for the finals. There had been concerns about terrorist attacks from the Montenaros, but the opening ceremonies went off without a hitch. Security was hardly in sight, quite unlike the 1974 World Cup in Germany, where rifles were visible (remember, this was just two years after the terrorist attack during the Munich Olympics), which had left a very bad taste, not only with the public, but also with the players themselves.

Argentina found itself in trouble almost from the opening of Group 1 play. Luis Cesar Menotti, the Argentine coach, angered the public and management by selecting no players from Boca Juniors, the club champions of Argentina, and he did not name seventeen-year-old Diego Maradona—acclaimed as the next Pele—to the final roster. Menotti, not so affectionately dubbed "El Flaco" by the fans, claimed that Maradona was too young. El Flaco was a lonely man, fighting the whole of Argentina.

No one envied Hungary, playing in the opener against the home team. The packed stadium cried, "Ar-chen-ti-na, Ar-chen-ti-na," but it was Hungary who struck early. Its center forward, Torocsik, was fouled three times in the first five minutes, but Hungary drew first blood on a goal by Csapo. Menotti just stared ahead. The Argentine fans were quiet, but not for long. Again, it was "Ar-chen-ti-na," and then, five minutes later, the equalizer on a free kick that the Hungarian goalkeeper could not hold. Luque raced in and scored. Both Hungarian stars, Torocsik and Nyilasi, were sent off the field for rough play, and Argentina's Bertoni scored the

A World Cup final duel between Luque of Argentina and Art Haan of Holland.

winning goal with only five minutes to go. Hungary's two carded players would have to sit out the next game. They could just about kiss their World Cup hopes goodbye.

In the France v. Italy matchup, it took France only thirty-one seconds for Lacombe to race downfield on the kickoff, take a pass from Didier Six, and head the ball past the great Italian goalie, Dino Zoff—the fastest goal scored in the World Cup since 1934. Thirty minutes later, the Italians equalized on a goal by Rossi, the highest dollar-valued player in the world. Then, seven minutes into the second half, Zaccarelli scored the winner. The Italians then handily match, 3–1. They were a shoo-in to advance to the next round.

It was France's turn to be at the not-so-tender mercies of Argentina's players and fans—77,000 of them jammed River Plate Stadium in Buenos Aires. Problems associated with sponsorship and endorsement of equipment appeared again in the French locker room—settled just before game time. The game was scoreless until just before halftime, when France's world-class sweeper, Tresor, applied a sliding tackle in the penalty area and inadvertently touched the ball with his hand. The Swiss referee, Jean Dubach, called it a penalty, although it really was not. Argentina's captain, Passarella, made the shot look easy. In the second half, French midfielder Platini tied the score. Didier Six had a one-on-one situation minutes later but slipped the ball wide past the post. Luque then hit a bomb from twenty-five yards out to put Argentina ahead 2–1, which held to the end.

The game between Italy and Argentina was billed as a match of cultural heritage. Argentina, with many people of Italian descent, was prepared to teach their "homeland" a lesson. Parking lots at River Plate Stadium were filled hours before the big event, but the game itself was rather dull. Neither team cared, as both qualified

Holland's Ernie Brandts (no. 22) beats the Austrian keeper Koncilia for the first of five goals for the Dutch in second-round competition at Cordoba. Holland went on to humiliate the Austrians 5–1.

Action during the World Cup final between Holland and Argentina in which the South Americans won 3–1 in overtime. Here Johnnie Rep of Holland leaps to head the ball above Passerella and Gallego (no. 6) of Argentina.

to the next round. The only thing at stake was the determination of where each team would play the next round. Italy turned out to be the unlucky one—they won 1–0 on a goal by Bettaga and advanced into the next round matched up with stiffer competition than Argentina. Catenaccio prevailed.

The Group 2 opener between West Germany and Poland was a game of tight defenses and very few chances taken, producing a scoreless tie. Cynics attacked the German coach, accusing him of making wrong selections and of being indecisive. They further criticized Germany's tactics and system. It was obvious that the Germans lacked leadership on the field. They had many good players but no one capable of taking charge. The aging Berti Vogts was preoccupied with Szarmach, and there was no Beckenbauer or Breitner or Müller. Helmut Schoen, the German coach, was torn between playing four midfielders, headed by Bonhof, or three front runners, lead by Rummenigge and Fischer. Germany's next game was against a young and inexperienced Mexican team—a cinch for Germany as they hammered home six goals, two each by Flohe and Rummenigge, and possibly thrusting themselves into a false sense of security.

Poland had its own problems. Coach Gmoch brought with him many players from the 1972 Olympic team and the 1974 third-place World Cup team—players like Lato, Deyna, Lubanski, Szarmach. But they were not the exciting team of 1974 and were lucky to win over Tunisia 1–0 and Mexico 3–1. Tunisia was the big surprise in this group. They were humble in their approach, stating early on that they had come to learn. They gave Germany a tussle and came away with one point in a scoreless game (the German press merely wanted the head of Schoen after that result). Then Tunisia beat Mexico 3–1—a good show. Mexico went packing early, winning no games, scoring only two goals, and allowing a total of twelve. There would be a change in Mexico when they returned home. Germany and Poland forged ahead, as predicted, but without impressing anyone.

Group 3's six games yielded only eight goals total. The main excitement, in fact, seemed to revolve around Brazil's lack of excitement. Its coach, Continho, not the favorite of the Brazilian public, had wanted to change the Brazilian style of play by introducing the Dutch style of "total soccer"—combining Brazilian skill and artistry with Dutch hard running and tackling. Good on paper, this plan was impossible to implement. It would take several generations to change the easygoing, music-loving "samba" type player into something different.

After Austria knocked off Spain 2–1, Brazil and Sweden played to a 1–1 tie, creating grumblings in Brazil. The Welsh ref, Thomas, disallowed a Brazilian goal as the final whistle sounded, claiming that it came after the whistle. Brazil protested, but to no avail.

In the second set of games, Austria again won by a goal—this time over Sweden 1–0—while Brazil tied (scoreless with Spain). Pele, doing TV commentary, buried the team, saying that their performance was worse than the 1966 World Cup. He couldn't understand what was happening to the Brazilian style of play. But the truth was that that style relied on superstars, and Brazil had no Pele, Didi, Vava, Tostao, Gerson, Jairzinho, Garrincha, etc. They had tried to make Zico the new hero, but he had a poor series. In their match with undefeated Austria, Brazil finally struck paydirt, winning 1–0 in a game of little interest, since both teams had already qualified through.

Austria was the surprise of the group. It quietly gained four points and was the leader of the group. Before arriving in Argentina, the Austrians had qualified via a win over the tough East Germans. Some experts had thought they would cause problems for the big guns in this Cup—and they did.

Austria brought its own superstar, Hans Krankl, the top scorer in the Austrian league. He upheld his reputation, scoring winning goals in a 2–1 victory over Spain and the 1–0 defeat of Sweden.

Group 4 produced some stormy moments as well. The Dutch team, the 1974 runnerup, arrived in Argentina with two managers, Zwartkruis and Ernst Happel. No one knew who was in charge. Probably neither one way—the players ran the show. Cruyff would not come to this one, even after much persuasion, 50,000 letters, and a hit record, "Oh Johan, Don't Leave Us in the Lurch." Van Beveren also refused to come, deciding that he did not want to travel. Several other big stars stayed away. But Holland was loaded with talent and fighting power players and came as the favorite in Group 4. They easily handled the dwarfed Iranians 3–0 on Rensenbrink's hat-trick.

Scotland had its own problems and couldn't put anything together until its last game against Holland. The team manager, Ally MacLeod, appeared to have stayed with the same team that got Scotland to the finals. His loyalty to certain players, however, was so strong that several seriously injured players traveled with the team to Argentina. These and other problems led to its disastrous World Cup performance. After a shocking 3–1 loss to Peru, the fans wanted MacLeod fired. Much unrest in the Scottish camp—but the press began to overdramatize some of the disturbances.

The second shocker followed the Peru game when Willy Johnston failed to pass the drug test routinely administered to two randomly selected players after each game. Johnston had taken some "pep pills" (fencamfamin), banned by FIFA. This incident made front pages all over the world, shaming the Scottish side and creating still a bigger problem for MacLeod. The Scottish F.A. banned Johnston for life and sent him home.

The unsettled and disorganized Scots then drew 1–1 with Iran. Now their only chance to prove their worth lay with hammering the Dutch. With much of the pressure removed, the team went out to demonstrate their true abilities, winning 3–2, finishing with an identical record as that of Holland but losing on goal difference and average. Strangely enough, MacLeod wasn't fired after all and remained as team manager after the Cup.

The aging Peru team, led by Cubillas, qualified but not as easily as it had appeared. They had encountered difficulty prior to their arrival in Argentina. The Peruvian Federation was broke, and FIFA had to loan it $100,000 to assure Peru's participation in the final sixteen. Peru also had to insure several of its top stars who had been playing abroad. For example, Sotil, playing in Spain, would be released only if a $500,000 insurance policy was taken out. Fortunately, Peru survived all these problems and picked up five points in the first round by beating Scotland, drawing scoreless with Holland, and trouncing Iran 4–1, with Cubillas scoring a hat-trick. It qualified at the top of Group 4.

The Group A opener between a dissension-racked West Germany and a rejuvenated Italy led to the Germans borrowing a page from Italian soccer history and going into the catenaccio bunker, playing for a tie. Two key West German players were injured, and possibly this was the reason for Helmut Schoen's tactics.

Italy, in contrast, came out swinging, Bettaga and Rossi being about as much as the Germans, led by Bertie Vogts, could handle. But the Italian defensive creation came back to haunt them. They couldn't penetrate the solid German defense, and the game ended 0–0.

After the final whistle, the West German players jumped for joy as though they had won the game. Schoen still believed that they would win their next game to reach the final. But the Italian manager Bearzot was not very pleased with the German tactics. He stated that his team had come not only to win the world championship but also to show attractive soccer to the world.

Meanwhile, the Dutch easily took Austria 5–1, putting the fear of God in both the German and Italian sides. Holland could do no wrong as Brandts, Rensenbrink, Rep (2), and Willy Van Der Kerkhof scored—and this without three regulars (Neeskens, Suurbier, and Rijsbergen). The Dutch were unsure as to whether to bring these players back for their next game, against West Germany. They chose to go with the team that had handled Austria so well. Germany scored within three minutes as Bonhof (noted as possessing the world's most powerful shot) took a free kick, which was blocked by the Dutch keeper but headed home by Ambramezik. In the twenty-seventh minute, Holland equalized on a thirty-

yard bomb by midfielder Arie Haan. It was the first goal allowed by German keeper Sepp Maier in 475 minutes of play.

A tie here would favor the Dutch rather than the Germans. The Orangemen played hard in the second half to avenge the memories of four years back. With twenty minutes to go, Dieter Muller put the Germans ahead on a header. Was history repeating itself? Then Willy Van Der Kerkhof's twin, Rene, got the equalizer, and the game ended in a draw. Holland needed only a tie with Italy to go through to the final. (Italy had successfully beaten Austria 1–0 to keep its hopes alive, but its goal difference was significantly behind Holland's, so it needed to beat the Dutch to go through.)

Now would Happel play his three injured players? He chose to use only Neeskens. Would the Italians be able to break the Dutch offside trap? They did—early in the game. Bettega outmuscled Brandts and, after the trap failed in the penalty box and with two players scrambling for the ball and the keeper Schrijvers coming out, Brandts got his foot to it first, pushing the ball through his own goal to give Italy a 1–0 lead. Schrijvers was injured on the play and had to be replaced by Jongbloed, whose spirit was willing but whose blood was thirty-seven years old.

Now Holland took over, Brandts redeeming himself with a twenty-yard equalizer. Then Neeskens pushed the attack forward to better utilize his hard running, strength, and power, and to confuse the Italian man-to-man marking. Arie Haan sent a thirty-yard bender under the crossbar to put

Holland ahead for good. Austria then nailed the German coffin shut with a 3–2 victory—the first time Austria had beaten Germany in forty-seven years—on two goals by Krankl and on an own goal by Vogts.

The Austrian victory knocked Germany out of the consolation game, and both teams went back to Europe on the same plane. Italy would play for third place from Group A.

Group B turned out to be Argentina and Brazil picking on Poland and Peru. Argentina's opener against Poland in Rosario featured the heroics of Kempes, who had been one of the few players that Menotti had invited from abroad. His early play in the Cup had been lackluster—enough for some to suggest that he be given his ticket back to Spain. But Menotti backed him up—and with good result as he scored in both halves in a 2–0 victory. Meanwhile Brazil overpowered the aging Peruvians 3–0, which caused Menotti not a little concern. Dirceu was Brazil's hero with two goals.

The big game of the group was the Brazil-Argentina confrontation, which was built up as the game to determine the world champion. The Latin press did not think much of the European opponents. But the game was boring with neither team showing anything that remotely warranted the title *world champion*. The principal excitement came from injuries (most notably to Argentina's Ardiles), and yellow cards (three to Brazil for rough play). The game ended in a scoreless draw.

Poland beat Peru 1–0 on a goal by Szarmach. Three days later it was Peru v. Argentina and Brazil v. Poland to determine which South American

neighbor would play in the final for third place. Brazil had complained from the beginning about the times of these matches. Their game against Poland was set for an earlier kickoff time, which would give Argentina an idea of how to set up tactics in their game (the big issue, after all, might well be goal difference). Moreover, Brazil made an issue of the fact that Quiroga, Peru's goalie, was born and raised in Argentina and might throw the game, accusing him of being bribed. This might have been true, considering the result of the Argentina-Peru game.

Brazil came out smoking against Poland, scoring on a twenty-five yard blast from Nelinho after thirteen minutes. Lato of Poland equalized before the half, but Roberto scored twice for Brazil in the second half. It appeared as though Brazil would be in the final (Argentina would have to beat Peru by four goals). The Brazilians went to the airport with transistor radios glued to their ears listening to the progress of the Peru-Argentina game.

But at 8:21 P.M. Luque scored his second goal to put Argentina ahead by 4–0—enough, unless Peru scored, to put Argentina in the final. Peru had some bites early in the game but after twenty minutes they were quiet. With Luque and Kempes doing gives-and-goes all evening, the Peruvian defense was in shambles. The result: 6–0, Argentina.

Argentina went wild; the scenes were unbelievable. The Brazilian press, as expected, went berserk, burying Peru. Headlines proclaimed the disgrace of Peru, its betrayal. The

Argentine press, just to keep the pot boiling, proclaimed the Brazil-Italy consolation game as the "losers final." They really know how to cement relations down there.

During the game for third place, Brazil was whistled throughout the entire game. Italy, which had beaten Argentina early on, was favored by the Argentine public. Italy opened the scoring midway through the first half, but then they fell back into their typical bunker, and the rest of the game belonged to Brazil, which started to bomb the Italian goalie from long distances. Brazil didn't score until the second half, but then they scored twice for the win. Brazil, the only undefeated team at the 1978 World Cup, finished third.

Both Argentina and Holland had been runners-up before—Argentina to its neighbor Uruguay in 1930 and Holland to its neighbor Germany in 1974. The sides looked even. The one big factor in favor of the Dutch was that their players would not return for the 1982 Cup—they would be too old. This would be their last opportunity. Argentina, of course, had an even larger advantage in being the home team.

It is normal to have one team or another make some kind of protest to upset its opponent, and sure enough, Argentina's captain, Passarella, protested to the referee about a small cast on Rene Van Der Kerkhof's right hand. The plaster had been there since his injury during the game with Iran. The referee, Sergio Gonella of Italy, was probably the wrong choice. He gave the impression that he was going to listen to anything, however unreasonable, anyone suggested. Van Der Kerkhof covered the cast with a soft padding, and the game was on.

After a first-half goal by Kempes, the second half belonged to Holland, although it was not until the eighty-second minute that Nanninga equalized on a header. But with little time remaining, Rensenbrink hit the woodwork, and the game had to go into overtime, where the momentum swung to the home team. Kempes struck again with the go-ahead goal, and Bertoni added another to make the final 3–1 for Argentina.

The 1978 World Cup was without the exceptional superstars. The participating countries played with caution—on the average, there were no more than two-and-one-half players on the attack, and these players often lacked finishing skills. Defense remained the byword.

1978 (Argentina)

GROUP 1

Italy (1)2	**France** (1)1
(Rossi, Zaccarelli)	(Lacombe)
Argentina (1)2	**Hungary** (1)1
(Luque, Bertoni)	(Csapo)
Italy (2)3	**Hungary** (0)1
(Rossi, Bettega, Benetti)	(Toth, A.)
Argentina (1)2	**France** (0)1
(Passarella, Luque)	(Platini)
France (3)3	**Hungary** (1)1
(Lopez, Berdoll, Rocheteau)	(Zombori)
Italy (0)1	**Argentina** (0)0
(Bettega)	

	GP	W	D	L	GF	GA	Pts
Italy	3	3	0	0	6	2	6
Argentina	3	2	0	1	4	3	4
France	3	1	0	2	5	5	2
Hungary	3	0	0	3	3	8	0

GROUP 2

German FR (0)0	**Poland** (0)0
Tunisia (0)3	**Mexico** (1)1
(Kaabi, Ghommidh, Dhouib)	(Vasquez Ayala)
German FR (4)6	**Mexico** (0)0
(D. Muller, H. Muller, Rummenigge 2, Flohe 2)	
Poland (1)1	**Tunisia** (0)0
(Lato)	
Poland (1)3	**Mexico** (0)1
(Boniek 2, Deyna)	(Rangel)
Tunisia (0)0	**German FR** (0)0

	GP	W	D	L	GF	GA	Pts
Poland	3	2	1	0	4	1	5
German FR	3	1	2	0	6	0	4
Tunisia	3	1	1	1	3	2	3
Mexico	3	0	0	3	2	12	0

GROUP 3

Austria (1)2	**Spain** (1)1
(Schachner, Krankl)	(Dani)
Sweden (1)1	**Brazil** (1)1
(Sjoberg)	(Reinaldo)
Brazil (0)0	**Spain** (0)0
Austria (1)1	**Sweden** (0)0
(Krankl)	
Spain (0)1	**Sweden** (0)0
(Asensi)	
Brazil (1)1	**Austria** (0)0
(Roberto)	

	GP	W	D	L	GF	GA	Pts
Austria	3	3	0	1	3	2	4
Brazil	3	1	2	0	2	1	4
Spain	3	1	1	1	2	2	3
Sweden	3	0	1	2	1	3	1

GROUP 4

Peru (1)3	**Scotland** (1)1
(Cueto, Cubillas 2)	(Jordan)
Netherlands (1)3	**Iran** (0)0
(Rensenbrink 3)	
Scotland (1)1	**Iran** (1)1
(Eskandarian. o.g.)	(Rowshan)
Netherlands (0)0	**Peru** (0)0
Peru (3)4	**Iran** (1)1
(Velasquez, Cubillas 3)	(Rowshan)
Scotland (1)3	**Netherlands** (1)2
(Dalglish, Gemmill 2)	(Rensenbrink, Rep)

	GP	W	D	L	GF	GA	Pts
Peru	3	2	1	0	7	2	5
Netherlands	3	1	1	1	5	3	3
Scotland	3	1	1	1	5	6	3
Iran	3	0	1	2	2	8	1

SECOND ROUND

GROUP A

German FR (0)0	**Italy** (0)0
Netherlands (3)5	**Austria** (0)1
(Brandts, Rensenbrink, Rep 2, W. van der Kerkhof)	(Obermayer)
Italy (1)1	**Austria** (0)0
(Rossi)	
Netherlands (1)2	**German FR** (1)2
(Haan, R. van der Kerkhof)	(Abramczik, D. Muller)
Netherlands (0)2	**Italy** (1)1
(Brandts, Haan)	(Brandts, o.g.)
Austria (0)3	**German FR** (1)2
(Vogts, o.g., Krankl 2)	(Rummenigge, Holzenbein)

	GP	W	D	L	GF	GA	Pts
Netherlands	3	2	1	0	9	4	5
Italy	3	1	1	1	2	2	3
German FR	3	1	0	2	4	8	2
Austria	3	1	0	2	4	8	2

GROUP B

Argentina (1)2	**Poland** (0)0
(Kempes 2)	
Brazil (2)3	**Peru** (0)0
(Dirceu 2, Zico)	
Argentina (0)0	**Brazil** (0)0
Poland (0)1	**Peru** (0)0
(Szarmach)	
Brazil (1)3	**Poland** (1)1
(Nelinho, Roberto 2)	(Lato)
Argentina (2)6	**Peru** (0)0
(Kempes 2, Tarantini, Luque 2, Houseman)	

	GP	W	D	L	GF	GA	Pts
Argentina	3	2	1	0	8	0	5
Brazil	3	2	1	0	6	1	5
Poland	3	1	0	2	2	5	2
Peru	3	0	0	3	0	10	0

THIRD PLACE GAME

Brazil (0)2	**Italy** (1)1
(Nelinho, Dirceu)	(Causio)

FINAL (Buenos Aires, 6/25/78)

Argentina (1)3	**Netherlands** 1
(Kempes 2, Bertoni)	(Nanninga)

Argentina: Fillol; Olguin, Galvan, Passarella, Tarantini; Ardiles (s. Larrosa), Gallego, Kempes; Bertoni, Luque, Ortiz (s. Houseman)

Netherlands: Jongbloed; Jansen (s. Suurbier), Krol, Brandts, Poortvliet; Neeskens, Haan, W. van der Kerkhof; R. van der Kerkhof, Rep (s. Nanninga), Rensenbrink

Referee: Gonella (Italy)

The Twelfth World Cup
Spain, 1982

sites: Madrid, Barcelona, Alicante, Seville, Vigo, Valencia, Bilbao, La Coruna, Elche, Malaca, Gijon, Oviedo, Valladolid, Zaragoza
109 entrants, FIFA membership 146

format: 6 groups of 4 each play round robin; 2 of each group go on to 4 groups of 3 that again play round robin; the 4 winners (semifinalists) play 1 game (group A v. C & B v. D) to determine finalists.

The challenge for the 11-pound solid gold trophy worth $4 million began after the opening festivities by five Spanish dancing groups and thousands of young athletes parading in the national colors of the twenty-four competing nations.

The Spanish organizing committee was pleased with the grand opening. The Barcelona's magnificent 120,000 Nou Camp Stadium was nearly full for the inaugural contest between Belgium and Cup holder Argentina on June 13.

After some nervous play, Belgium settled down, and Erwin Vandenbergh, the former European scoring champ, got the world cup started in a new direction. A pass from teammate Alex Czerniatynski landed on Vandenbergh's foot, and the crowd of 95,000 waited in silence to see if tradition would be broken. Ever since the single opening game was instituted back in 1966—five World Cups ago—it had always ended in a scoreless tie. The Argentine goalkeeper Fillol raced out to cut the angle, but the cool Vandenbergh confidently hammered the ball past the unsure goalie and into the back of the

net. Adios tradition! The underrated Belgium team, a 28–1 shot by the London bookies, had humiliated one of the most respected powers of the world. The Belgians deserved to win, for they created more opportunities. The Argentine offsides trap had five or six breakdowns, and on three other occasions a Belgian player could have improved the 1–0 lead. It was surprising to see Argentina apply the trap on occasions when it was difficult to execute, particularly in the shooting area where the opponent is playing one-two's.

The Argentines showed some life in the last fifteen minutes and Diego Maradona's free kick off the crossbar rebounded to Kempes, who was unsuccessful in finishing. The final score remained 1–0 for Belgium—a good indication of what was to come.

The Third World came with blind confidence, thinking they could prove themselves worthy of being in the final competition. Many upsets and surprises were evident during the first ten days of play. The shocking result of Algeria upsetting powerful West Germany in

Group 2 by 2–1 had the German coach Derwall chain-smoking for days. Even though West Germany dominated play, Algeria countered only twice and made good on both occasions. The Cameroon tied each of its opponents in Group 1. Unfortunately, they did not advance to the next round due to the Italians' superior goal average. Kuwait in Group 4 did some barking as well, as they demonstrated that they could hold their own with the European and Latin American powers. The Kuwaiti prince threatened to pull the team off the field if the referee allowed a goal scored by the French to stand. In an embarrassing moment for FIFA, the Soviet ref disallowed the goal. But the French went on to win 4–1, and the next day it was goodbye ref and the Kuwait Federation was fined $11,000 for their actions.

Kuwait offered special bonuses to its players for victories—unheard of before in World Cup play. They stung

West Germany's **Wolfang Dremmler** and France's **Michel Platini** exchange friendly shoves during their dramatic semifinal game.

the soccer rich East European power Czechoslovakia with a 1–1 tie. A controversial penalty awarded to the Czechs saved some embarrassment for the Slovaks. Jubilant with a tie, 3,000 Kuwaiti fans danced in the streets of Valladolid, many of them in long robes and others in vests bearing the motto "Our camel is a winner." The Kuwaiti players were promised $200,000 if they were to reach the next round. Honduras did well in representing the CONCACAF Region, tying host Spain and Cameroon. El Salvador after a 10–1 humiliation by Hungary redeemed itself, losing 1–0 to Belgium and Argentina.

In Group 5, Honduras surprised the host, battling the Spaniards to a 1–1 tie. A questionable penalty awarded to Spain in the last fifteen minutes did not sit well with the visitors nor the visiting audience. It was only in Group 6 that the games and results went according to prediction. After the completion of the first round, the performance of the Third World countries had the Spanish sportswriters calling the week-old world championship the "rebellion of the modest," delighting in the refusal of these underdog soccer nations to be taken for granted by the mighty of the sport. It certainly vindicated the FIFA president, Dr. Havelange, who insisted the twenty-four nation concept. The upset performance by Algeria, Kuwait, Honduras, and Cameroon against established European soccer powers had rattled the oddsmakers in London and enchanted the nervous organizers of the tournament in Spain; they are now convinced that increasing the number of teams from sixteen to twenty-four was, after all, a good idea.

The Algerian victory over Germany had the people of Algeria pouring into the streets in an explosion of patriotic horn honking and embracing that had last occurred when the embattled nation gained its independence from France over twenty years ago.

National pride fell low in West Germany along with its powerful side, who had won all eight of its qualifying matches by scoring 33 goals and allowing only three.

So the first round of play was an emotional and exciting one for the newcomers in World Cup competition. Their traditions, costumes, and culture, along with playing performance, added another dimension to the greatest sporting event in the world. The superpowers showed very little. Poland, Italy, Germany, Yugoslavia, and Czechoslovakia did not impress; they demonstrated little marked improvement in their play over previous years. The expectations of the 1.5 billion people viewing around the world were not fulfilled by the soccer powers. The world-class players were disappointing as well. Rummenigge, Boniek, Maradona, Rossi, Blokhin, Platini, Nehoda, and Susic all played below their capabilities. Brazil was the only nation that demonstrated that theirs is another level of play in world competition, and if it were not for them, the soccer world would have been easily fooled. Attacking football can be played if

there is a willingness on the part of the players and coaches. Brazil expressed offensive play with speed, skill, and finishing. Eder's winning goal against the Soviet Union was by far *the* goal of the first round. With two minutes remaining, he collected a pass outside the eighteen-yard area—Socrates running a "dummy" (stepping over the moving pass)—chipped the ball up with his left foot and, without breaking stride, took a full volley with the same foot and packed it in the upper ninety, the calm Soviet goalie looking on. There were other great goals by the Brazilians, but none to match Eder's. It was thanks to Brazil for the first round play that kept the spirits of the soccer world alive. The big question in the back of this writer's mind was whether they could continue to play with the same enthusiasm and mental energy for the remainder of the tournament.

Meanwhile, Germany and Austria were whistled for ninety minutes in their game. After Germany scored in the early going of the first half, both teams decided to finish out at midfield. Germany needed to win and Austria could afford to lose by one goal to advance. Algeria cried foul, for they could have advanced if Germany tied or lost. Needless to say, the match was the most boring of all the games played in the first round. Later FIFA reprimanded both countries for their poor performance.

After the big surprises, celebrations, and question marks about Third World performances,

Action (?) during the Germany-France semifinal.

there is nothing like the real thing. After convincing victories over the Soviet Union and Scotland, the spectacular Brazilian team, with a bench stronger than most of its rivals, was labeled *awesome*. Team manager of New Zealand, John Adshead, after the game against Brazil stated, "It was like playing a team from the twenty-first century." When the final scores and standings were tabulated and the emotions left the stadiums, the bottom line remained practically the same. The teams most likely to advance to the next round advanced. As the French newspapers wrote: "And now for the real act." The powers of the soccer world now had to show their true qualities. In the second round, the four groups of three were aligned accordingly:

Poland	West Germany
Soviet Union	England
Belgium	Spain
Italy	France
Brazil	Austria
Argentina	Northern Ireland

The first game of each of the groups was critical, for the survivor had a good chance of advancing to the semifinals.

Poland opened against Belgium and displayed some big-time soccer, memories of their 1974 play in Germany. They outclassed the Belgium

Goalkeepers of the finalists: On the left is Italy's Dino Zoff and on the right West Germany's Harald Schumacher.

team 3–0 as the Polish superstar, Boniek, collected a hat-trick. The Soviet Union could only muster a 1–0 victory over the Belgium squad, setting up a politicaal game between the Poles and the Soviet Union. The Soviet Union needed to win by at least two goals for a shot at the semis, but the Poles were too good and actually outplayed their rivals, the Poles, settled for a scoreless tie and a spot in the final four. The Soviet Union went packing, while Poland celebrated the result as a victory for Solidarity. On this occasion, some 300 Polish fans in Spain for the games defected to the free world.

In group B, West Germany battled hard to win over Spain by a narrow margin of 2–1. Diminutive Pierre Littbarski did it all for Germany as he scored the first goal and assisted in the winner. This set the stage for the England v. Germany showdown. The two nations having tremendous respect for each other decided to battle it out at the midfield, and the boring game resulted in a scoreless draw. The only excitement was generated in the last five minutes of play when Rummenigge of Germany hammered a cannon from thirty-five yards against the crossbar, catching the English keeper Peter Shilton only looking. But a rebound doesn't count, and the score remained 0–0. Shilton set the record for keeping—426 scoreless minutes. England was now in the driver's seat; it had to beat Spain by a two-goal difference to advance. England and Brazil were the only two teams unbeaten to this point. However, the English lacked scoring punch, and the now-healthy Keegan could not help put England in the final four. It was the last trip for Manager Ron Greenwood, but the team had put forth a valiant effort. In his report on English soccer, he wrote that the young English players need to learn man-to-man marking at an early age because their learning first played with team speed that was hardly seen throughout the tournament by any other nation. Attacking back Junior demonstrated what wing play is all about as he rushed forward at will, finally scoring a goal to ice the victory for Brazil. At midfield, it was Falcao who controlled and set the rhythm for Brazil. His ability to go forward from deep midfield and score goals added another dimension to this dynamic team. In the attack, Zico, Socrates, Serginho, and Eder were dangerous at all times. They humiliated Argentina 3–1, but the result was not indicative process would be more concentrated and their skills could improve much more rapidly. Assuming responsibility at an early age is a great carryover into the player's soccer growth and maturity.

In group C, the strongest of the matchings, included Brazil, Argentina, and Italy. To the surprise of all soccer fans, Italy went out against Argentina and demonstrated that—yes—they can score goals despite their low-scoring performance in the first round. They outclassed the gauchos of Argentina 2–1 on goals by Tardelli and Cabrini, giving the Italians a deserved victory and a shot at the samba-playing Brazilians. It was up to Brazil to drive the nail into the coffin of world-champion Argentina. Brazil played with team speed that was hardly seen throughout the tournament by any other nation. Attacking back Junior demonstrated what wing play is all about as he rushed forward at will, finally scoring a goal to ice the victory for Brazil. At midfield, it was Falcao who controlled and set the rhythm for Brazil. His ability to go forward from deep midfield and score goals added another dimension to this dynamic team. In the attack, Zico, Socrates, Serginho, and Eder were dangerous at all times. They humiliated Argentina 3–1, but the result was not indicative of the game. Brazil, on this day, was six goals better. The young superstar, Maradona, near the end of the game, received a red card for dirty play and was ejected with minutes remaining. It was not a good way to finish—his had been a disappointing performance, particularly for the Barcelona Club of Spain that reportedly paid $6–8 million for his services. They believed that they had overpaid, and who would quarrel with them? The stage was set in Group C with Brazil, full of confidence, taking on the resurrected Italian *azzuri* squad. In a game that shook the world—and in particular Brazil—the Italians prevailed with a 3–2 victory. The Italians took an early lead over Brazil—noted for their slow start—Rossi of Italy capitalizing. Socrates then equalized for Brazil. Soon, it was Rossi again as "Johnny on the Spot," lifting the score 2–1 in favor of the Italians. In the second half, Falcao equalized for Brazil. However, Rossi came through with a hat-trick—result, Rossi 3, Brazil 2. Rome and other cities in Italy went into a wild frenzy of jubilant celebration. The Fountain of Trevi was filled with Italian fans celebrating in mad hysteria, while the mood in Brazil bordered on despair. Eleven cases of suicide were reported in Rio de Janeiro, higher than the one-per-day average. Sao Paulo had a record number of people in hospitals receiving treatment for nervous disorders and stress.

So the dynamic Brazilian team, which had performed so well, could not sustain the long-enduring tournament. Italian Manager Bearzot was hailed in Italy as a tactical genius. The truth of the matter was that Brazil decided to play soccer for ninety minutes and had not fallen into a heavy defensive posture. They could have advanced on a 2–2 draw due to goal average. The fact remained that several faulty clearances by Brazilian defenders led to several Italian goals.

In group D, France had an easy time with Northern Ireland and Austria. They defeated Austria 1–0, but deserved better. Against the Irish it was hardly a contest as the French demonstrated a high level of skill through the individual flair of Platini, Six, Tigana, and a defensive block of Tresor and Bossis. After a disappointing performance against England, the French redeemed

themselves and showed that they can play with anybody in the world. They were full of confidence going into the semifinals.

In the semi, the matchups were Poland v. Italy and West Germany v. France. With the exception of France, the other three countries had roster problems. Key players such as Rummenigge for Germany, Boniek for Poland, and Gentile for Italy would not be able to play. Rummenigge had hamstring problems and had not played against Spain in the second round.

The Italians—bubbling with enthusiasm and confidence after two of the greatest victories in their World Cup play history—came out smoking against Poland. Poland played very tentatively without Boniek, having drawn 0–0 with Italy in their first-round game. When you take your team leader off the field, you take a goal away from the team. The result was clear for Italy. Rossi again became the hero, scoring a goal in each half. Kupcewicz of Poland hit the woodwork on a free kick from thirty five yards out, and that's as close as Poland came to scoring. Rossi now took over the leading scorer position with a total of five goals in the competition. So now the Italians were looking at the France-Germany game, and Rome was going wild again as people hit the streets with noisemakers, horns honking, church bells ringing, another celebration. Before the game against Germany, Platini of France remarked that the French team under Manager Hidalgo had a plan to beat Germany. Without Rummenigge, the Germans were at best an average team.

Even with the team captain, they were struggling all along and did not display the form that had won them the European Cup. Pierre Littbarski opened the scoring for Germany, but the French did not panic, displaying some excellent soccer and, for the most part, outplaying Germany. If the French had a weakness then, it was in goalkeeping. They equalized on a Platini penalty kick, and the score stayed 1–1 at the close. West Germany had several close encounters but failed to capitalize. Since it was the semifinal round, a winner had to be determined. Therefore, two fifteen-minute periods were played after the tie. Should the game remain tied in overtime, each team would take penalty kicks to determine the winner.

In overtime the French looked as though they would run the Germans off the field. In 102° heat, France struck in the sixth minute. A free kick taken by Giresse from the right side outside the penalty area was served high into the box on the ten-yard line. Tresor, who pushed up into the West German box, took it on the full volley and hammered it past Schumacher, the German goalie—a great goal and the French had 2–1. Immediately, the injured Rummenigge began to warm up on the sideline, and shortly after he was inserted into the game. But the French came roaring out again. A

The scoring heros of the World Cup were West Germany's Karl-Heinz Rummenigge, who was injured with a pulled hamstring during the games, and Italy's Paolo Rossi, who came back from a two-year suspension for knowing about fixed games and from a lackluster initial round to lead the Azzuri to victory and win the scoring crown.

twenty-yard drive by Giresse, set up by Didier Six, gave France a 3–1 lead.

The true mark of a great team shows when a team is down by two goals with only eighteen minutes remaining in overtime and comes back to equalize. The reason for the German revitalization was their captain Rummenigge. As he stepped on the field, a new life and fighting spirit rose among the Germans. He immediately went to work creating danger in the French penalty area. Finally, he pushed the ball wide to the left and made a near-post run to score, narrowing the lead to 3–2. In the second overtime it was all West Germany, as they pushed the French into the French penalty area. Finally, the tying goal came on a scissors kick by Fischer over the head of the goalie and a French defender. The game ended in a 3–3 draw. The penalty-kick method was the next phase to break the tie. Never before had a semifinal ended thus. The tension mounted as players from each team took turns shooting from the 12-yard penalty spot. It was 3–2 favor the French when French keeper Jean-Luc Ettori punched clear the normally reliable Uli Stielike's shot. Stielike sank to the ground inconsolate. But soon French veteran Didier Six had his shot saved by Schumacher to square matters at 4 apiece. Schumacher then stopped Maxine Bossis and Horst Hrubesch chinched the victory for the Germans.

Rummenigge had proven in eighteen minutes that he was world class and possibly the best front runner in the world. Having the talent and ability to go both ways, offensive and defensive, and the soccer knowledge of midfielder makes him very unique. Coach Derwall

was hailed as the supergenius who had timed Rummenigge's insertion into the game perfectly. Had the Germans lost, he would have been accused of being an idiot for keeping Rummenigge on the bench so long. That, of course, comes with coaching. The French team, falling into a defensive posture after a two-goal lead, could have contributed to their elimination from the finals. Allowing Rummenigge, even though injured, to run free without marking him was a big surprise to knowledgeable soccer fans. For certain, the Italian marksman Gentile would be on Rummenigge like in the final. Unfortunately, it was a big letdown to the French. Coach Hidalgo and the team should be proud, for they displayed quality soccer, and Tresor, their sweeper, showed that he can play both ways as he pushed forward relentlessly against the Germans.

The second round proved to be more exciting and the superpowers of the soccer world showed better. A European World Cup final will not sit well with the Latins; for them its back to the drawing board. With the exception of Brazil and Argentina (of European extraction), the Latins need much work, for they play too show. More often than not, each player touches the ball too many times before playing it to a teammate to advance the ball.

The consolation game of Saturday, July 10th, played between Poland and France was the typical "who cares? We let the big one slip away." Poland prevailed as Boniek was back in the lineup, and the Poles played with more assertiveness. Platini of France, for reasons unknown, decided not to play.

The final score, 3–2 for Poland, gave the Eastern European country a third place in the World Cup, the same as they achieved in 1974, when they defeated Brazil, 1–0.

The showdown between Italy and Germany had everyone guessing as to who would be the favorite. The Italians had the momentum while the Germans demonstrated against France that their game was coming back, particularly with Rummenigge in the lineup again. It would be a battle between the hot-scoring Rossi and the injured Rummenigge to bring out a result. Rossi was now the hero of the *azzuri*. His two-year suspension for having knowledge of games being fixed in Italy was all forgotten. All is forgiven when you perform and win for the motherland. Rummenigge indicated that he would play regardless of his hamstring pull.

The game started with West Germany having more of the play. The Italians appeared to be intimidated. They did not come out smoking as they did against Argentina and Brazil. After some twenty minutes and Germany unable to find gaps to set up goal chances, the game was quiet. Neither team displayed any flair to go forward, and it was very apparent that the first half would end in a draw. However, the Italians had something else in mind, and a curving ball was passed into the German penalty area, and the German defender was forced to take down an onrushing Italian forward from the right. A penalty was awarded by the Brazilian referee, and it appeared that Italy would make it 1–0.

Italy's magic moment in the World Cup final, Rossi (center, falling to the ground) has just headed home the first goal past Schumacher, while Antonio Cabrini looks on excitedly.

The victorious Italians.

Not so, as Cabrini missed—it was the first missed penalty shot in World Cup—the first ever in a final. The first half ended 0–0.

In the second half, the Italians survived the agony of the missed shot and recovered to defeat Germany 3–1. This victory gave the Italians their third title, equaling Brazil. The hero was again Rossi as he scored the first goal on a header from a pass by Gentile. Tardelli and Altobelli were the other goal scorers. It was not until the eighty-third minute tha Breitner scored for Germany. Rossi, the storybook hero, was the leading scorer for the cup with six goals.

The Italian players carried their captain, the forty-year-old Dino Zoff, on their shoulders after the victory. The aging veteran was an inspiration to the World Champions. In a surprise move by manager Bearzot, the young eighteen-year-old Bergomi received the monumental task of marking Rummenigge; he did a fine job. The five-goal scorer Rummenigge was substituted by Hansi Muller in the seventieth minute.

Rome again was in full swing as thousands of Romans staged a delirious victory celebration. Legions of banner-waving fans marched, sang, and chanted their way through the historic center of Rome, the traditional route of triumph granted to ancient Rome's victorious generals. Wine and champagne corks popped as Italians saluted one another and toasted their team. The final game was not artistic by any means. Rough play prevailed and the Brazilian referee was busy issuing yellow cards to Conti, Oriali, Dremmler, and Stielike. Italy deserved to win, they did not win by a fluke but very convincingly. They won their last three games against possibly the three strongest soccer nations in the world.

Germany never showed their form. They advanced from the beginning as a result of luck. Finally, luck ran out, and they could not hold their own against Italy. In general, very few innovative ideas of modern soccer were on display. Most teams showed up with the same traditional tactical patterns of their country. Brazil was the only nation that demonstrated remarkable progress from the teams fielded in 1974 and 1978. Their players demonstrated high skill execution at full speed, more so than any other country.

All the other expectations for the World cup were fulfilled. Emotional stress, suicides, despair, players' cars destroyed—that's the other side of the World Cup. Criticism by national newspapers about their teams' performance, in Austria, the USSR, and Belgium was on par with stories of past World cup play. Coaches criticized by newspapers and many *fired* and still to be replaced are other results that continue the World Cup tradition. As our saying goes, the 1982 World Cup is history.

With anticipation and trepidation the world soccer population awaits the next World Cup to be staged in Colombia in 1986. We shall see what soccer will look like four years from now as the many countries that entered will go through self-analysis in the hope of being there.

1982 (Spain)

Group 1

| Italy | (0)0 | Poland | (0)0 |

| Peru | (0)0 | Cameroon | (0)0 |

| Italy (Conti) | (1)1 | Peru (Diaz) | (0)1 |

| Poland | (0)0 | Cameroon | (0)0 |

| Poland (Smolarek, Lato, Boniek, Buncol, Wlodzimierz) | (0)5 | Peru (La Rosa) | (1)1 |

| Italy (Graziani) | (0)1 | Cameroon | (0)1 |

	GP	W	D	L	GF	GA	Pts
Poland	3	1	2	0	5	10	4
Italy	3	0	3	0	2	2	3
Cameroon	3	0	3	0	1	1	3
Peru	3	0	2	1	2	6	2

Group 2

| Algeria (Madjer, Belloumi) | (0)2 | German FR (Rummenigge) | (0)1 |

| Austria (Schachner) | (1)1 | Chile | (0)0 |

| German FR (Rummenigge 3, Reinders) | (1)4 | Chile (Moscoso) | (0)1 |

| Austria (Schachner, Krankl) | (0)2 | Algeria | (0)0 |

| Algeria (Assad 2, Bensaoula) | (3)3 | Chile | (0)2 |

| German FR (Hrubesch) | (1)1 | Austria | (0)0 |

	GP	W	D	L	GF	GA	Pts
German FR	3	2	0	1	6	3	4
Austria	3	2	0	1	3	1	4
Algeria	3	2	0	1	5	5	4
Chile	3	0	0	3	3	8	0

Group 3

| Belgium (Vandenbergh) | (0)1 | Argentina | (0)0 |

| Hungary (Kiss 3, Nyilasi 2, Fazekas 2, Poloskei, Toth, Szentes) | (3)10 | El Salvador (Zapata) | (0)1 |

| Argentina (Maradona 2, Bertoni, Ardiles) | (2)4 | Hungary (Poloskei) | (0)1 |

| Belgium (Coeck) | (1)1 | El Salvador | (0)0 |

| Belgium (Czerniatynski) | (1)1 | Hungary (Varga) | (0)1 |

| Argentina (Passarella, Bertoni) | (1)2 | El Salvador | (0)0 |

	GP	W	D	L	GF	GA	Pts
Belgium	3	2	1	0	3	1	5
Argentina	3	2	0	1	6	2	4
Hungary	3	1	1	1	12	6	3
El Salvador	3	0	0	3	1	13	0

Group 4

| England (Robson 2, Mariner) | (1)3 | France (Soler) | (1)1 |

| Czech (Panenka*) | (1)1 | Kuwait (Al-Dakhil) | (0)1 |

| England (Francis, Barmos, o.g.) | (0)2 | Czech | (0)0 |

| France (Platini, Six, Genghini, Bossis) | 4 | Kuwait (Buloushi) | 1 |

| France | 1 | Czech | 1 |

| England (Trevor) | (1)1 | Kuwait | (0)0 |

	GP	W	D	L	GF	GA	Pts
England	3	3	0	0	6	1	6
France	3	1	1	1	6	5	3
Czechoslovakia	3	0	2	1	2	4	2
Kuwait	3	0	1	2	2	6	1

Group 5

| Honduras (Zelaya) | (1)1 | Spain (Ufarte*) | (0)1 |

| Yugoslavia | (0)0 | N Ireland | (0)0 |

| Spain (Gomez*, Saura) | (1)2 | Yugoslavia (Gudelj) | (1)1 |

| N Ireland (Armstrong) | (1)1 | Honduras (Laing) | (0)1 |

| Yugoslavia (Petrovic*) | (0)1 | Honduras | (0)0 |

| Spain | (0)0 | N Ireland | (0)0 |

	GP	W	D	L	GF	GA	Pts
N Ireland	3	0	3	1	1	1	3
Spain	3	1	2	0	3	2	4
Yugoslavia	3	1	1	1	2	2	3
Honduras	3	0	2	1	2	3	2

Group 6

| Brazil (Socrates, Eder) | (0)2 | USSR (Bal) | (1)1 |

| Scotland (Wark 2, Dalglish, Robertson, Archibald) | (3)5 | New Zealand (Sumner, Wooddin) | (0)2 |

| Brazil (Zico, Oscar, Eder, Falcao) | (1)4 | Scotland (Narey) | (1)1 |

| USSR (Gavrilov, Blokhin, Baltacha) | (1)3 | New Zealand | (0)0 |

| Scotland (Jordan, Souness) | (1)2 | USSR (Chivadze, Shengelia) | (2)2 |

| Brazil (Zico 2, Falcao, Serginho) | (2)4 | New Zealand | (0)0 |

	GP	W	D	L	GF	GA	Pts
Brazil	3	3	0	0	10	2	6
USSR	3	1	1	1	6	4	3
Scotland	3	1	1	1	8	8	3
New Zealand	3	0	0	3	2	12	0

Group A (Second Round)

| Poland (Boniek 3) | (2)3 | Belgium | (0)0 |

| USSR (Organesyan) | (0)1 | Belgium | (0)0 |

| Poland | (0)0 | USSR | (0)0 |

	GP	W	D	L	GF	GA	Pts
Poland	2	1	1	0	3	0	3
USSR	2	1	1	0	1	0	3
Belgium	2	0	0	2	0	4	0

1982 (cont.)

Group B

| German FR | (0)0 | England | (0)0 |
| German FR | (0)2 | Spain | (0)1 |

(Littbarski, Fischer) (Zamora)

| England | (0)0 | Spain | (0)0 |

	GP	W	D	L	GF	GA	Pts
Germany	2	1	1	0	2	1	3
England	2	0	2	0	0	0	2
Spain	2	0	1	1	1	2	1

Group C

| Italy | (0)2 | Argentina | (0)1 |

(Tardelli, Cabrini) (Passarella)

| Brazil | (1)3 | Argentina | (0)1 |

(Zico, Serginho, (Diaz)
Junior)

| Italy | (2)3 | Brazil | (1)2 |

(Rossi 3) (Socrates, Falcao)

	GP	W	D	L	GF	GA	Pts
Italy	2	2	0	0	5	3	4
Brazil	2	1	0	1	5	4	2
Argentina	2	0	0	2	2	5	0

Group D

| France | (1)1 | Austria | (0)0 |

(Genghini)

| N Ireland | (1)2 | Austria | (0)2 |

(Hamilton 2) (Pezzey, Hinter-
maier)

| France | (1)4 | N Ireland | (0)1 |

(Giresse 2, Roche- (Armstrong)
teau 2)

	GP	W	D	L	GF	GA	Pts
France	2	2	0	0	5	1	4
Austria	2	0	1	1	2	3	1
N Ireland	2	0	1	1	3	6	1

Semifinals

| Italy | (1)2 | Poland | (0)0 |

(Rossi 2)

| German FR | (1)(3)4 | France | (1)(3)3 |

(Littbarski, Rum- (Platini, Tresor,
menigge, Giresse)
Fischer,
Hrubesch†)

† Kicked the deciding penalty shot

In the Shootout:

| German FR | (5)5 | France | (4)4 |

(Littbarski, Kaltz, (Giresse, Amoros,
Breitner, Rumme- Rocheteau, Platini)
nigge, Hrubesch)

Third Place Game

| Poland | (2)3 | France | (1)2 |

(Szarmach, Majew- (Girard, Couriol)
ski, Kupcewicz)

Final (Madrid, 7/11/82)

| Italy | (0)3 | German FR | (0)1 |

(Rossi, Tardelli, (Breitner)
Altobelli)

Italy: Zoff; Bergomi, Scirea, Collovati,
Cabrini; Oriali, Gentile, Tardelli; Conti,
Rossi, Graziani (Altobelli, Causio)

German FR: Schumacher; Kaltz, Stielike, K.
Foerster, B. Foerster; Dremmier
(Hrubesch), Breitner, Briegel; Rummenigge
(Mueller), Fischer, Littbarski)

Referee: Coelho (Brazil)

*Penalty-shot goal

Scoring Leaders for World Cup Tournaments

1930 Stabile (Argentina) 8; Cea (Uruguay) 5; Subiabre (Chile) 4

1934 Nejedly (Czechoslovakia), Conen (Germany), and Schiavio (Italy) 4

1938 Leonidas (Brazil) 8; Zsengeller (Hungary) 7; Piola (Italy) 5; Williamowski (Poland), Sarosi (Hungary), and Wetterstroem (Sweden) 4

1950 Ademir (Brazil) 7; Schiaffino (Uruguay) and Basora (Spain) 5

1954 Kocsis (Hungary) 11; Morlock (German Federal Republic) and Probst (Austria) 6; Hugi (Switzerland) 5

1958 Fontaine (France) 13; Rahn (German Federal Republic) and Pele (Brazil) 6; Vava (Brazil) 5

1962 Jerkovic (Yugoslavia) 5; Albert (Hungary), Garrincha (Brazil), Ivanov (USSR), Sanchez (Chile), and Vava (Brazil) 4

1966 Eusebio (Portugal) 9; Haller (German Federal Republic) 5; Beckenbauer (German Federal Republic), Hurst (England), and Porkujan (USSR) 4

1970 Müller (German Federal Republic) 10; Jairzinho (Brazil) 7; Cubillas (Peru) 5; Pele (Brazil) and Byshovets (USSR) 4

1974 Lato (Poland) 7; Szarmach (Poland) and Neeskens (Netherlands) 5; Rep (Netherlands), Edstroem (Sweden), and Müller (German Federal Republic) 4

1978 Kempes (Argentina) 6; Rensenbrink (Netherlands) and Cubillas (Peru) 5

1982 Rossi (Italy) 6; Rummenigge (West Germany) 5; Boniek (Poland), and Zicc (Brazil) 4

World Cup Team Standings through 1982 Games

Country	Starts	1 (5 pts)	1 (4)	3 (3)	4 (2)	Final Round (1)	Total
Brazil	12	3	1	2	1	5	32
West Germany	10	2	2	2	1	3	29
Italy	10	3	1	0	1	5	26
Uruguay	7	2	0	0	2	3	17
Argentina	8	1	1	0	0	6	15
Hungary	8	0	1	1	1	4	13
Sweden	7	0	1	1	1	4	13
Czechoslovakia	7	0	2	0	0	5	13
France	8	0	0	1	1	6	11
England	7	1	0	0	0	5	11
The Netherlands	4	0	2	0	0	2	10
Yugoslavia	7	0	0	1*	1	5	10
Austria	5	0	0	1	1	3	8
Chile	6	0	0	1	0	5	8
Mexico	8	0	0	0	0	8	8
Poland	4	0	0	2	0	2	8
Spain	6	0	0	0	1	5	7
Switzerland	6	0	0	0	0	6	6
Belgium	6	0	0	0	0	6	6
USSR	5	0	0	0	1	4	6
USA	3	0	0	1	0	2	5
Scotland	5	0	0	0	0	5	5
Bulgaria	4	0	0	0	0	4	4
Peru	4	0	0	0	0	4	4
Portugal	3	0	0	0	0	3	3
Romania	3	0	0	0	0	3	3
Paraguay	3	0	0	0	0	3	3
Northern Ireland	2	0	0	0	0	2	2
Bolivia	2	0	0	0	0	2	2
El Salvador	2	0	0	0	0	2	2

Norway, New Zealand, Egypt, Cuba, Dutch East Indies, South Korea, North Korea, Turkey, Wales, Colombia, Israel, Morocco, East Germany, Australia, Zaire, Haiti, Tunisia, Algeria, Honduras, Cameroon, and Kuwait all have competed once and have 1 point.

*In 1930, there was no third-place game. In goal difference, the United States won third place, but both the U.S. and Yugoslavia go down as third-place winners here.

III

The U.S. National Teams and the World Cup

THE UNITED STATES HAS COMPETED IN THE FINAL ROUND OF THE WORLD CUP ON three occasions. Unfortunately, very little growth and development of the sport resulted. On the contrary, soccer suffered in that the losses soured the American public. Were it not for the American ethnic clubs, soccer might well have disappeared from the American sports scene. Other countries, because of their participation in the World Cup, were building long-standing traditions of playing other nations and of developing soccer players on a yearly basis who would become world class players. The United States was not so fortunate.

The 1930 team consisted of six ex-British professionals, plus a sprinkling of other ethnic players. They easily won their first two matches, defeating Belgium and Paraguay by identical scores of 3–0. The next round, against Argentina was not quite the same. Some experts chose the U.S. as the favorite based on the two previous results. Initially, it looked good as the British players' fighting spirit and mobility held Argentina to a 1–0 lead at halftime. The second half was another story, however, and Argentina scored three goals within a nine-minute spell, breaking the U.S. team's resistance. Argentina's Stabile then went on to score two more goals, giving his country a 6–1 victory.

In the 1934 World Cup in Italy, the Americans became the sparring team for the host nation. With Mussolini

watching the opening game, declaring that his country would win the World Cup, Italy demolished the U.S. squad 7–1. It must be remembered that teams did not have to qualify for these early cup games—the finals were open to all.

The U.S. did not take part in the 1938 World Cup because of domestic problems. Then came the 1950 World Cup, the last time a U.S. team had participated in the final round. In this World Cup, the U.S. team left a bit of history behind by upsetting the famed English squad at Belo Horizonte, Brazil.

The United States had had feeble results against Mexico, losing to them twice prior to their arrival in Brazil. However, the Americans did defeat Cuba, and it was by virtue of this win that they entered the final round.

Opening against Spain, they put up a good fight before losing 3–1. No one expected them to do anything against the favored English squad, loaded with stars like Matthews, Milburn, and Ramsey who took the Americans lightly.

The American team was made up of a combination of native-born Americans and some newly acquired

90

naturalized U.S. citizens. Among the former were Matt Bahr and Harry Keough. (Bahr is the head soccer coach at powerful Penn State, while Keough is the coach of the famous soccer power, St. Louis University). Both players played important roles in the American victory over England. Keough defended, and Bahr assisted on the winning goal that came from the head of the Haitian-born Gaetjens. The British public could not believe the score. Many news media publications were swamped with phone calls from people who wanted to check the accuracy of the reported score. To this day, there are discussions on why England lost.

The United States Soccer Federation continued to enter teams in the preliminary qualifying rounds of the CONCACAF region. The teams were never organized properly or sufficiently prepared for the competition. A coach would be appointed by the USSF Board, but this was usually a political appointment. The major obstacle that confronted the U.S. teams in their quests to reach the finals came from its friend south of the border, Mexico. The United States team could never overcome the Mexican squad.

For the most part, very few people cared about the National Team results or their performance in World Cup qualifying rounds. The American public was uninformed and indifferent. The ethnic Americans and new immigrants supported their native countries. It was merely an exercise to enter U.S. teams in order to maintain membership and good standing with FIFA.

A serious effort, however, was put forth in the mid-sixties by the USSF president, James McGuire, to select a team and coach and make a strong attempt to qualify for the 1966 World Cup in England. Geza Henni, along with George Meyer, were appointed coaches, and through a winter of regional trials a team was selected in March 1965. Henni had a good coaching record with the New York Hungarians, members of the New York German-American League. He was a top goalie prior to the Hungarian revolution. Following the revolution, he settled in New York as a player/coach with the New York Hungarians. His team's victories over several top Mexican teams convinced McGuire that his experience would help the U.S. finally qualify over Mexico.

The team assembled in Bermuda for training prior to departure for the home-and-home matches with Mexico and Honduras. Training sessions were feeble with little organizational sense applied. George Meyer used his marine fitness act, and Coach Henni ran the 8 v. 8 practices.

The team played four matches against local Bermuda clubs and all-star teams. The results were encouraging, and the U.S. team began to look organized. Coach Henni explored possible systems and finally decided he would use a 4–2–4 formation—the one Brazil had made famous.

Bob Kehoe was the captain. The other players were mostly naturalized citizens, with six players coming from the New York Hungarian squad. Willie Roy (coach of the Chicago Sting), yours truly, Eddie Murphy, Al Zerhusen, Helmut Bicek, and Walt Schmotolocha were the forwards.

The first game against Mexico was a good result with a 2–2 draw. Played at the Los Angeles Coliseum in front of some 35,000 Mexican spectators screaming "Viva Mexico!," the U.S. team took a 2-1 lead on a goal by Schmololocha from a free kick. However, the Canadian referee, Morgan, awarded a feeble penalty to Mexico against the U.S. goalie, Victor Gerley. The Mexicans equalized and were happy with the draw. They knew the return match in Mexico would be a different story. The American squad too was happy, but realized that a tie at home would not be sufficient, for a victory in Mexico City was very unlikely. Honduras had lost 2-0 to Mexico a week earlier.

The U.S. departed for Mexico City to play its next game at the newly built University Stadium. At an altitude of 7,800 feet, visiting players have difficulty just running. The Americans lost 2-0 and appeared to be through unless Honduras could pull off an upset.

The two games played against Honduras were both played in that country for financial reasons. The U.S. defeated Honduras 1-0 in San Pedro Sulla, while they tied 1-1 in Tegucigalpa. Mexico defeated Honduras again 2-0 and went on to England.

The next attempt to reach the final appeared to be somewhat easier. Since the 1970 World Cup was hosted by Mexico, they were an automatic qualifier. This allowed for still another CONCACAF representative in the final sixteen. With Mexico out of the picture, things looked brighter for the U.S. squad.

The problem, however, was that there was no continuity. The team that

had played in 1965 had been disbanded, and no system for the development of players had been created. A new coach, Phil Woosnam, was appointed, along with Gordon Jago. This period in American soccer development marked the beginning of full-time professional leagues. The NPSL (National Professional Soccer League) was the first American league; it had ten franchises and an abundance of foreign-bought talent, with a sprinkling of Americans such as Pat McBride (coach of the Kansas City Comets), Carl Gentile (of the St. Louis Stars), and myself. I was then playing for the Philadelphia Spartans, owned by the Rooney family (owners also of the Pittsburgh Steelers).

The local trials for this team were poor. The word from the top was that most of players would be younger, preferably under twenty-six years of age. Very few players from the 1965 squad, which had come close to qualifying, made the team. Yet the 1969 squad was formidable; among its talented players were Bob Gansler (currently the assistant coach of the U.S. National Teams), Adolf Bachmier, Ed Murphy, Peter Millar, Willie Roy, Vic Gerley, Nick Krat, and Ziege Stritzell.

But the team had a slow start, losing to Canada 4-2. In the return match at home, the U.S. reversed the result, taking the Canadians 1-0. Bermuda was the next opponent, and the U.S. had no difficulty in handling the small tourist island, defeating them twice, 5-2 and 2-0.

In the next round, it was Haiti that the Americans had to face. Phil Woosnam had resigned as coach prior to the games against Haiti to accept a position as Commissioner of the North American Soccer League. This obviously did not help the U.S. team and was reflected in the disappointing results—losses of 2–0 and 1–0 and the consequent elimination from the competition. El Salvador survived from the CONCACAF region and went on to join the final sixteen.

In 1973, the U.S. was again starting over with new coaches and new players, but it was an exercise in futility, proving that the U.S. must come up with a better approach.

Bob Kehoe and Gene Chyzowych were appointed coaches. The selection of players this time around was mostly on paper. The professional league was struggling. Woosnam was working hard to keep it alive. There were very few players in the league that could help the National Team effort.

Several tours were organized to expose the team to international competition. However, there was no continuity to the list of players who joined each tour—it was always a different group. Werner Roth, Barry Barto, Al Trost, Pat McBride, Nick Krat, and Bob Rigby were some of the players who made up the nucleus of the team. One week of preparation time in the Catskills, with some players only available on the day of the game, did not help the coaching staff.

There were some exciting moments in that year as the U.S. squad upset Poland at Hartford, Connecticut, 1–0, on a goal by Al Trost—a fine victory for the U.S. and acting coach Gene Chyzowych. However, this glory was short lived; Canada and Mexico had an easy time disposing of the Americans.

The U.S. lost to Mexico 3–1 at Azteca Stadium in Mexico City in front of 91,000 spectators and lost again in the return match in the United States 2–1. Canada won its home game against the Americans 3–2. A 2–2 draw with Canada in the U.S. knocked the Americans out of the running.

With the arrival of Pele, a newly born interest on the part of young Americans created a soccer boom. With this excitement, a more serious attempt was made to prepare the U.S. National Teams. A search committee was appointed to recommend a full-time national coach. Dettmar Cramer was the choice. His experience as assistant coach with the West German National Team in Mexico in 1970 would give him the edge in finding a way to defeat the Mexicans. He stayed for six months and left behind a very well outlined coaching scheme that only needed implementation, a defeated Olympic team and several losses by the National Team to Mexico. The USSF, still determined to regain the services of Cramer, tried very hard, and a legal battle almost ensued between the USSF and the Bayern Munich Soccer Club. The issue was finally resolved by having Bayern Munich play several matches in the U.S. Based on the recommendation of Dettmar Cramer, I was hired as the second full-time national coach.

This was in August of 1976, and the U.S. team was to play in the qualifying matches in October and November against Canada and Mexico. With assistance from the NASL office, and Phil Woosnam's assurance that the NASL clubs would cooperate by making players available for

competition, the player selection process began; it was a process that insured that players who played more minutes for their respective clubs in NASL games had a better chance of making the National Team (in other countries, selection is based on outstanding performance—not minutes played). Of the twenty-two members chosen, fourteen arrived on September 14th for training in Colorado Springs. Following the NASL's Soccer Bowl, the other selected players arrived. The training consisted of two-a-days at the Air Force Academy.

After several scrimmages in the Denver area, the team embarked on a three-week, five-game tour to Colombia, Peru, Ecuador, and Venezuela as a preparation for the upcoming trials against Mexico and Canada. Ours was a young team, with little international experience and a distinct lacking in quality forwards. The team concentrated on organizing a solid defense and building a high intensity level of play. A 2–1 loss in Bogota, Colombia, against club team Millionaros was a good beginning. Two ties in Peru, a 1–0 loss in Ecuador, and a 2–0 loss in Venezuela were hardly embarrassing and served to add some confidence to the young players.

Upon returning from South America, the team traveled to Seattle, Washington, to train for a week on AstroTurf prior to the Canadian match in Vancouver. Some of the Cosmos players joined the team at this point, including Bob Smith and Shep Messing. Messing, however, decided to return home after the Canadian game. Mausser and Meyer had the edge on Shep in goal at this time, and Shep saw

that there was no need for three goalkeepers.

A good result for the U.S. team—the Canadians were lucky to gain a tie in the second half, after Steve Pecher (St. Louis Steamers) was ejected for abusive language. Boris Bandov scored the goal for the Americans. The team had earned one solid point toward qualification. Next stop: Los Angeles Coliseum against Mexico.

The team arrived at the Coliseum two hours before kickoff. It was obvious that a large Mexican crowd would be at the game, but no one expected over 40,000 Mexicans on this sunny afternoon. While entering the player gate with the two vans, the stadium guard intervened and would not allow the vans to enter because we had no passes. I then instructed the vans to back up and return to the Hilton Hotel. With this, the guard realized that maybe it was the U.S. team. Fearing a Mexican revolution if the game was not played, he reluctantly allowed us to enter. Some beginning for the Americans—playing in their own country, supposedly on their home field! To rub salt into the wound, our team was shown into the visiting locker room, while the Mexicans were escorted to the plush locker room used by the Los Angeles Rams. It was a bit of added fuel for the American players. They were already making plans behind the scenes to strike if conditions and salaries were not improved.

Despite the added aggravations, the U.S. team fought hard. The defense was at its best, stopping the Mexican raids inspired by the very vocal Mexican crowd. Arnie Mausser was in good form, along with Alex Skotarek,

David D'Errico, and Jim Pollihan. Neil Cohen stopped Cuellar (San Diego Sockers), while Al Trost tried to hold the middle of the field for the Americans. Near the end of the game, Grgurev and Bandov had chances to give the U.S. a lead but missed. The final score was 0–0.

Now, with two points toward qualification, things looked promising. The next day, the squad boarded a plane back to Colorado Springs for further altitude training in preparation for the upcoming qualifier in Mexico City. It was long flight from Los Angeles to Denver. The players were seated in 'thrift' class. Signs of an impending strike were on everyone's faces. Sure enough, upon arrival in the Springs, the players voted to strike. The coaches attempted to persuade the team not to strike, but we failed. Major newspapers in the U.S. and around the world jumped at the opportunity to write about the strike. Ironically, very few papers had carried the result of the U.S.-Mexico game, much less a story about it. The strike was better print.

It was a three-day strike, with negotiations being conducted over the telephone with USSF leaders, who were apparently on soccer-related business in London. They had got wind of the strike from an article in a London daily. The issues were finally resolved—the players received raises in their weekly salaries, plus bonuses for winning and tying. The scars remained, however, and the spirit and comaraderie that was built up over the previous six weeks disappeared.

The team left for Mexico City a day prior to the game. A first-class hotel helped ease the resentment. But the ritual of Mexican promises, very seldom fulfilled, was ever present. The bus that was to take us to the training ground arrived one hour late. Upon arriving at the field, the gate was locked, and the players were forced to climb the wall. The team had a thirty-five minute workout before darkness set in—hardly enough. We were told the game would be played at noon the next day. Prior to departure, the kickoff time was changed to 3 P.M. Upon arriving at the stadium at 1:30 P.M., the Canadian referee, in a rush, informed us that we had thirty minutes to prepare for kickoff, which was apparently now at 2:00 P.M. After a frantic dressing and taping scene in the American locker room, the team made the official kickoff time without a warm-up and was down 2–0 within twenty minutes.

Well, the game was over. You don't score on Mexico when they are winning by a good goal margin. In the second half, Steve Pecher was kicked in the head and suffered a mild concussion—we finished with ten players. A ridiculous penalty called by the Canadian referee with little time remaining on the clock gave the Mexicans a 3–0 victory and a good goal average. This penalty would eventually force a playoff between the Canadian and U.S. teams and eliminate the Americans from qualifying into the next round.

The last and final stop for the U.S. team was to be the Kingdome in Seattle for the last game of the series, between the U.S. and Canada. Mexico had lost to Canada 1–0 in Vancouver, so the U.S. chances to move into the next round looked favorable. We had to win by two goals in Seattle, and Canada would have to lose in Mexico. The late Miro Rys (who was killed the following year in an auto accident while en route to training with a German Bundesliga team) was the American hero as the nineteen-year-old scored the first goal for the Americans in front of 18,000, mostly American, fans. It was a good feeling for the American squad. Julie Veee scored the second goal, and it appeared as though the U.S. would be in the next round, provided Canada lost to Mexico. A third goal by Boris Bandov was disallowed by the Mexican referee, and the score stood 2–0 for the U.S.

Luck would not be with the U.S. side, as Canada pulled off a 0–0 tie in Mexico. That tie forced the three teams into a three-way tie, each team having four points. Mexico advanced on goal average. However, Canada and the U.S. were deadlocked on goal average as well, necessitating a playoff—according to FIFA rules, on a neutral field.

Haiti was the site chosen for the playoff between the two countries. The U.S. team reassembled early in December and played games in Aruba, Curaçao, and Surinam before arriving in Haiti. Canada, in the meantime, prepared in Central America.

The U.S. team lacked scoring power (as was evidenced in their games against the Netherlands' Antilles Islands) but was confident from its recent win over Canada. On the day of the game, team captain Al Trost had a fever and would be of limited service. The Canadian team showered the Haitian fans with roses before kickoff, immediately placing themselves in their good graces (an idea of John McMahon, the Canadian team manager). The game

was not one of artistic beauty, as both teams, very tense, demonstrated little skill or tactical thought. The U.S. made some early raids on the slow Canadian defense, however Bandov, Flater, and Grgurev were not on target. A deflected goal off Trost gave Canada that all-important first goal. The U.S. team tried hard in the second half, without Trost and without success. Bobby Smith was the standout for the Americans, John Lenarduzzi for Canada. Steve Pecher again received walking papers early in the second half, leaving the team with only ten. With ten minutes remaining in the game, a header by Bandov from a serve by Bob Smith was missed. With only two minutes in the game, Lenarduzzi did a solo to make it 2–0. A thirty-yard "bomb" with fifteen seconds remaining and the U.S. defense desperately pushing forward, gave Canada a 3–0 victory.

The work to prepare a 1981 team started four months later. A young, under-21 team was assembled to play the Dutch Olympic team on the West Coast. A 2–0 victory and a 2–1 loss convinced the national coaches that the young Americans could, indeed, compete with the amateurs of the world. The big question was how to make them professionals. We moved players up into the ranks as quickly as possible. Gary Etherington and Ricky Davis were the first two to join the senior squad, along with Greg Villa and Tony Bellinger. These players did well as the U.S. team won the Festival of the Americas, a USSF-hosted tournament in New York with club teams from Peru, Colombia, and Ecuador. Allianza of Peru showed up with Soltil and Cubillas—two great internationals. This

team was not even enough to keep the Americans down. Greg Villa, with four goals, was the MVP of the tournament, as the U.S. won 3–0, 2–0, and 2–1 over the Latin sides.
Greg Villa, with four goals, was the MVP of the tournament, as the U.S. won 3–0, 2–0, and 2–1 over the Latin sides.

Dividends began to pay off—the young Americans were learning quickly. Many were being wooed into the NASL clubs. Initially we were all excited for the young players. But the potential experience to be gained never panned out; the Americans warmed the NASL benches.

The USSF national coaching staff was doing its best to weed out and identify the top American talent. We wanted more Ricky Davises, more Greg Villas, Ty Keoughs, and more Tony Bellingers immediately. We knew, however, that it would take time to develop this type of talent.

The USSF agreed to keep as many young Americans on amateur forms as possible, and initially the pro leagues cooperated. The purpose in keeping players on amateur status was that it provided many more opportunities for exposure to international play, i.e., the Pan Am Games, the Olympics, and, for some, the World Youth Championships. It was a good idea on paper, but in practice it didn't work.

Pro clubs, in the heat of their seasons, were reluctant to release players for international play. This became a major headache for all concerned. The National Team coaching staff was frustrated by not having players available for training. The pro people were irritated by the

international scene. They were concerned about their investment first. The players were caught in the middle. The potential of having top players available for international competition became a farce. Some team heads refused to answer phone calls, others would not open the USSF letters requesting players, and still others would not send players until the day of the actual competition. This shuttling of players for the U.S. National Team existed in 1976 and is still present today.

The Americans were giving all concerned with the National Team the much-wanted hope they were looking for. A classic show in Bellinzona by the young Americans was talked about all over Europe. The Pan American team qualified for the Pan Am games (Bermuda, April 1979) via a win over Mexico, and a tie with Canada. Again, players were shuttled from one airport to another on the first day of the event. Nevertheless, the teams were winning.

Wins over the Mexican Olympic team in Bermuda and the Los Angeles Coliseum had the Mexicans concerned. Our amateurs had the upper hand. The rejuvenated American team had a decent showing in Seattle against the Soviet Union, losing 3–1, with Ricky Davis scoring for the U.S. It was no longer the haphazard, disorganized, one-week-prior-to-departure appointment of a national coach. There was now a plan in place to build a team raised by the system. The scheme was working, and many a soccer cynic was disturbed, for they were failing, or had already failed, drastically with soccer in America. As the days were nearing for the 1981 qualifications, the pro clubs became less and less cooperative. The

World Cup Competition U.S. National Team Results

Date	Opponent/Score	Site/Country
July 13, 1930	U.S. 3, Belgium 0	Montevideo, Uruguay
July 17, 1930	U.S. 3, Paraguay 0	Montevideo, Uruguay
July 26, 1930	Argentina 6, U.S. 1	Montevideo, Uruguay
May 24, 1934	U.S. 4, Mexico 2	Rome, Italy
May 27, 1934	Italy 7, U.S. 1	Rome, Italy
Sept 4, 1949	Mexico 6, U.S. 0	Mexico City, Mexico
Sept 14, 1949	U.S. 1, Cuba 1	Mexico City, Mexico
Sept 18, 1949	Mexico 6, U.S. 2	Mexico City, Mexico
Sept 21, 1949	U.S. 5, Cuba 2	Mexico City, Mexico
June 25, 1950	Spain 3, U.S. 1	Curitiba, Brazil
June 29, 1950	U.S. 1, England 0	Belo Horizonte, Brazil
July 2, 1950	Chile 5, U.S. 2	Recife, Brazil
Jan 10, 1954	Mexico 4, U.S. 0	Mexico City, Mexico
Jan 14, 1954	Mexico 3, U.S. 1	Mexico City, Mexico
Apr 3, 1954	U.S. 3, Haiti 2	Port-au-Prince, Haiti
Apr 4, 1954	U.S. 3, Haiti 0	Port-au-Prince, Haiti
Apr 7, 1957	Mexico 6, U.S. 0	Mexico City, Mexico
Apr 28, 1957	Mexico 7, U.S. 2	Long Beach, California
June 22, 1957	Canada 5, U.S. 1	Toronto, Canada
July 6, 1957	Canada 3, U.S. 2	St. Louis, Missouri
Nov 6, 1960	U.S. 3, Mexico 3	Los Angeles, California
Nov 13, 1960	Mexico 3, U.S. 0	Mexico City, Mexico
Mar 7, 1965	U.S. 2, Mexico 2	Los Angeles, California
Mar 12, 1965	Mexico 2, U.S. 0	Mexico City, Mexico
Mar 17, 1965	U.S. 1, Honduras 0	San Pedro Sula, Honduras
Mar 21, 1965	U.S. 1, Honduras 1	Tegucigalpa, Honduras
Oct 17, 1968	Canada 4, U.S. 2	Toronto, Canada
Oct 27, 1968	U.S. 1, Canada 0	Atlanta, Georgia
Nov 2, 1968	U.S. 6, Bermuda 2	Kansas City, Missouri
Nov 10, 1968	U.S. 2, Bermuda 0	Hamilton, Bermuda
Apr 20, 1968	Haiti 2, U.S. 0	Port-au-Prince, Haiti
May 11, 1969	Haiti 1, U.S. 0	San Diego, California
Aug 20, 1972	Canada 3, U.S. 2	St. John's, Canada
Aug 29, 1972	U.S. 2, Canada 2	Baltimore, Maryland
Sept 3, 1972	Mexico 3, U.S. 1	Mexico City, Mexico
Sept 10, 1972	Mexico 2, U.S. 1	Los Angeles, California
Sept 24, 1976	U.S. 1, Canada 1	Vancouver, Canada
Oct 3, 1976	U.S. 0, Mexico 0	Los Angeles, California
Oct 18, 1976	Mexico 3, U.S. 0	Puebla, Mexico
Oct 20, 1976	U.S. 2, Canada 0	Seattle, Washington
Dec 22, 1976	Canada 3, U.S. 0	Port-au-Prince, Haiti
Oct 25, 1980	U.S. 0, Canada 0	Ft. Lauderdale, Florida
Nov 1, 1980	Canada 2, U.S. 1	Vancouver, Canada
Nov 9, 1980	Mexico 5, U.S. 1	Mexico City, Mexico
Nov 23, 1980	U.S. 2, Mexico 1	Ft. Lauderdale, Florida

Top: The 1964 U.S. team at Randalls Island, New York, just before its match with the 1966 world champion English team (Walt Chyzowych is in the first row on the right); Bottom: The U.S. squad of 1965 (Chyzowych, first row on the right).

success of the NASL clubs in the mid- to late seventies had attracted the eyes of the soccer community. The National Team was a nuisance to the pro clubs. Little did they realize that the ultimate success of soccer in America will depend upon the performance of our National Teams in the World Cup.

Despite the roadblocks, the USSF continued with its efforts to field a formidable team. The U.S. Olympic team was made up of players who had remained amateur in the pro leagues and top players from the high school and collegiate ranks. It was important for the Olympic team to do well, for many of these players would be moving up to the National Team. Victories over Bermuda home (5–0) and away (3–0) showed that the team had an excellent chance of reaching Moscow. There was, however, a bit of a setback for the U.S. when Ricky Davis decided to turn professional after the second game against Bermuda. The contract offered by the New York Cosmos was too good to be refused.

Nevertheless, the team continued to have success, gaining five points in the final round of qualifications for the CONCACAF region. A victory over Surinam in Orlando, Florida, on March 16, 1980, coupled with an all-important win in Costa Rica on March 20 (in front of 23,000 hostile fans), iced a trip for the Americans to Moscow. It was only the second time in U.S. soccer history that a U.S. team qualified for the Olympics (Bob Geulker, the coach at S.I.U.-Edwardsville, had taken the U.S. team to Munich in 1972). Little did the team know that President Carter would cancel the flight to the Soviet Union.

The final preparation for the 1980

World Cup qualifiers was a successful tour of Europe, with victories in Spain and Belgium. A major upset over the Hungarian National Team in Budapest by a score of 2–0 had the soccer world looking at the U.S. team's performance. Louie Nanchoff and Angelo DiBernardo were the goalgetters, while Makowski, Pecher, Bellinger, and Keough controlled the defense.

The qualifying games against Mexico and Canada were scheduled for October and November. A home-and-home series was announced by the USSF, with the U.S. slated to open its competition in Ft. Lauderdale against Canada. A preparation tour was organized for the team. After a training period at the Adidas Sports Hotel in Germany, the team continued on to play F.C. Nuremberg and Arminia Bielefeld, both of the West German Bundesliga, the Luxembourg National Team, Portuguese National Team, and the English "B" Team.

It was during this time that a repeat of the 1976 player strike occurred. After several meetings while on the European tour, they informed me prior to the Luxembourg game on October 4 that unless the federation met their terms, they would not play the remainder of the tour. After a series of phone calls from Kurt Lamm and myself to the president of the USSF, Gene Edwards, we finally convinced him that the players were very serious about not finishing the tour—much less playing in the World Cup qualifiers—if their requests were not discussed and settled. Both Edwards and Werner Fricker, the senior vice-president of the federation, arrived in Bielefeld to help resolve the situation. Negotiations, involving three player representatives, Greg Makowski, Ringo Cantillo, and Steve Pecher, and the federation people, lasted until one hour before kickoff, and still the issue was unresolved. The U.S. team lost to Arminia Bielefeld that evening 5–3. Then it was back to the bargaining table. Negotiations continued until 5 A.M., and on two occasions Harry Weisz, the equipment manager, was instructed to collect the players' equipment and make arrangements for the U.S. team's departure to the U.S. Finally, I made the decision to go to each team member, posing the question of whether they would stay under the new conditions being offered. One young player offered, from his own pocket, the difference needed in order to settle the strike. It was a patriotic gesture, but one that was never considered. It was at this point that the players decided not to expose themselves individually—the vote was split at nine for staying, and ten for leaving. They requested another five-minute meeting alone and voted to accept the new terms and continue playing. In retrospect, the strike and the lengthy tour of Europe prior to the qualifying games were major contributing factors in the demise of the U.S. team.

Two good results against Luxembourg (a 2–0 victory) and Portugal (a 1–1 tie) gave the team confidence. A fair result against the English "B" team—a 1–0 loss—had the team on its way back to the U.S. Throughout the European tour, players were being shuttled back and forth, playing for their club teams (which were on tour at the time) one evening and returning to play for the U.S. team the next evening in another country. Some of the American players from the Cosmos did not even join the squad until the last game of the tour. It could have been an embarrassing moment during the Nuremberg game had Arnie Mausser been injured, since there was no backup goalkeeper. Winston DuBose was playing with his club team at the time in England.

Following a week of training in Ft. Lauderdale, the opening game against Canada, played on October 25th at Lockhart Stadium, proved to be disappointing. Even though the U.S. dominated play, scoring opportunities missed by Liveric, Davis, and Makowski resulted in a 0–0 tie. In the return match in Vancouver's Empire Stadium, the U.S. team played tentatively and lost all enthusiasm to win. Canada scored a good goal on a header by Iarusci. With only minutes to halftime, the Latin referee awarded a questionable penalty kick to Canada. With the score now 2–0, the U.S. came back fighting. However, the team was only able to generate one goal—a header by Greg Villa from Ricky Davis.

The next game, played in Azteca Stadium in Mexico City at noon, produced a result the Mexicans had wanted for years—a 5–1 blowout. The game started with a Mexican raid on the American goal that pinned the U.S. team on their own twenty-yard line. The 93,000 Mexican spectators were enjoying every minute. It appeared as though the U.S. team would hold out until halftime. However, in the thirty-first minute, during a Mexican corner kick, Steve Pecher was kicked by a Mexican player. No foul was awarded, and the game continued. While Pecher was being attended to by trainer Steve Parker, the U.S.—now shorthanded—could not hang on. Four goals fell in a matter of nine minutes.

The second half was peaceful, and the pace was tempered with each team scoring one goal. Ricky Davis scored from a penalty kick after Louie Nanchoff was taken down in the penalty box. There was little hope for the U.S.'s survival into the next round.

In the last game of the tournament, the U.S. played Mexico at Ft. Lauderdale. There was nothing at stake for the Americans except for their pride. They played with heart, outclassing the Mexican team and giving the Americans their first victory ever over Mexico in World Cup qualifying games. Steve Moyers of the New York Cosmos was the hero of the match with two goals. Ricky Davis converted to sweeper for that particular game, due once again to a shortage of players.

The Americans had failed again, this time with the best available young native talent and the longest preparation time of any previous U.S. National Team. But it was a great learning experience. Let us hope that the USSF will not make the same mistakes again. Some things to remember might include:

1. The preparation for the U.S. National Team should be held in one concentrated geographical area and should not include plane-hopping from one country to another. The U.S. team lost its much-needed enthusiasm after the European tour.

2. At all costs, player strikes should be avoided. The last U.S. squad was divided in their own discussions during negotiations, and this division took its toll on the field.

3. Never allow executives from pro clubs into the locker room following a qualification game. One particular individual showed up with three air tickets following the U.S.-Canada game in Ft. Lauderdale. His players were expected to join their club, which was on tour. Fortunately, they refused to leave.

4. A policy must be developed regarding the availability of National Team players at all levels. A good number of coaches refused cooperation—not only on the pro level but on the college and high school levels as well.

5. Settle all problems related to equipment endorsement prior to team arrival. Discussing what shoes a player must wear ten minutes before kickoff is hardly the proper time or place.

6. The practice whereby players join the U.S. squad on the day of game, following a night of travel and club game, must be stopped.

7. When players are with the U.S. National Team, they must remain with the team until the tour/tournament is completed.

8. U.S. team preparation and international exposure should be continued in Europe.

Playing in Central America, where stadia are primitive and conditions are unsafe, is of no physical benefit to the U.S. player. It was a great learning experience for Ricky Davis and Gary Etherington to play for the U.S. against an El Salvadorian club team in Santanna, a small town outside San Salvador. The stadium, old and rudimentary, and the locker rooms, without shower facilities or a roof, were eye openers for the young Americans. After a 1–0 victory for the U.S., and fisticuffs between Greg Villa and the opposing team, the U.S. squad had a difficult time making their way into the underground tunnel leading to the locker room. The decision was to send one player at a time, so that the smallest possible target would be offered for the rocks thrown by spectators. The bricks tossed over the wall of the roofless dressing room made changing difficult, so the players remained in their warmups for the return trip to San Salvador. (Years earlier, near the town of Santanna, a soccer war took place when El Salvador and Honduras could not settle their score on the field. They finished it with tanks and bullets.)

9. A minimum of seven days preparation time should be mandatory before any international game. Playing France at Giants Stadium without even a team meeting certainly contributed to the devastating 6–0 catastrophe.

10. The continuity of the National Team programs must be sustained. Exposing young players to the outside world is an all-important factor in their growth and development. The philosophy and methods established in the early seventies for developing American players must be continued.

IV
The U.S. National Youth Team in Youth World Cup Play

N ADDITION TO THE SENIOR SQUAD, THE OLYMPIC TEAM, AND THE PAN AM TEAM, the United States Soccer Federation is also responsible for organizing and preparing the U.S. National Youth Team for international competition. The first serious attempt to expose young American players to international play came in July 1975, when a team was selected to compete in Canada in the CONCACAF regional tournament.

The coaches appointed to handle the team were George Logan of San Diego State University and Timo Liekoski, coach of Hartwick College (Timo later also coached the Houston Hurricane, Edmonton Drillers [NASL], and the New Jersey Rockets [MISL]). There was no system for the selection of players. Most were political, determined by state associations or by those individual coaches around the country who had bothered to make recommendations. The two coaches hardly had the time necessary to scan the country looking for the best player talent. The USSF Youth Division had the greatest amount of input, with the players typically being chosen from those state associations with the largest youth membership.

The full complement of the youth team arrived at Hartwick College for six days of training prior to departure for Canada. The team trained twice a day, with the coaches trying—as efficiently as was humanly possible—to mold the team into a cohesive unit. A large number of the players came from St.

Louis, the "hotbed of soccer," headed by the technically sound Ty Keough and his roommate, Larry Hulcer, both midfielders. Greg Makowski, Don Aubachon, and Neil Cohen of Dallas were other St. Louis area players; all later graduated to bigger and better things, playing professional soccer.

In the course of those six days, the youth team had two scrimmages against a group of coaches who were attending a USSF coaching school at Hartwick. The two scrimmages were hardly sufficient competition for the young players, especially when you consider that most of the coaches were semifit and over the hill.

The team left for Canada and, surprisingly enough, was competitive in every game. They defeated Guatemala 2–1 and tied Cuba 0–0. They then went on to tie Trinidad 1–1, only to lose on penalty kicks, knocking them out of the running. They did, however, come up with one more victory as they defeated Jamaica 2–0 in a consolation game. Not a bad showing at all. From this group of players came some very important members of the U.S. National Team.

The intention of the USSF to field a

National Youth Team for competitive international play was, and is, a good one. However, the selection and preparation must be conducted on a highly professional level. During Dettmar Cramer's six-month tenure, he prepared an Olympic team, which traveled to Israel, and the senior National Team, which played several games against Mexico. His results were as predicted—no wins. Those who had had experience working with soccer in America knew that, regardless of his credentials, no single coach could turn soccer around 180° in such a short amount of time.

On August 1, 1976, I accepted the position of U.S. national coach and resigned as associate professor and soccer coach at Philadelphia Textile College. Within two weeks, both the National Youth Team and the senior National Team had to be prepared for World Cup qualification. It was obvious that I could not be in two places at the same time; a youth coach was needed who could select and train the youth team for the CONCACAF tournament hosted by Puerto Rico.

Ray Klivecka (New York Cosmos, Buffalo Stallions) was appointed, with Angus McAlpine as assistant. Once again, the lack of time made player selection difficult. Through recommendations from various coaches around the country, some thirty players were invited to train at Boca Raton College in Florida. After a week of training and observation, the squad was cut down to eighteen players.

The team traveled to Puerto Rico for the first Youth World Cup qualifications. It was an exciting time in U.S. soccer history to see how the young American players would fare under this type of international competition. The team was housed in an old U.S. military base—with barracks certainly looking worse than they did during World War II. In the height of the summer, late August and September, the heat and humidity are unbearable in Puerto Rico. In the barracks, without air conditioning, it was even more impossible. The temperature ranged from 110°F to 120° F. Under conditions such as these, optimal performance could hardly be expected. Despite the horrible housing and the cow-pasture–converted practice fields, the U.S. Youth Team did very well. They finished in third place, behind Mexico and Honduras.

The U.S. won its first three games without much difficulty, defeating Bermuda 3–0, Nicaragua 1–0, and the Dominican Republic 9–0. The true test came against Mexico. It was here that the U.S. team could not handle the mature, skilled Mexican team, going down 7–1. The team rebounded and played an inspired game against Canada, winning 4–2. The victory moved them into the semifinals. However, a 1–0 loss to Honduras in a hard-fought contest (where the deciding goal was a questionable one) kept the team from reaching the final round in Japan. In playing for third and fourth place, the U.S. team went on to defeat Guatemala 1–0.

It was a great learning experience for all concerned and, in particular, for the young players. They began to understand how the international game is played—the gamesmanship, the officiating, the opponent and their tactics, the fair play(?), and the pressures of winning and being successful. Most of these players learned well and went on to become better players as a result. Some cried and found they couldn't cope with the conditions or the pressure. Some others weren't talented enough for the international standards. So the group was weeded out, and many who survived the test are now good professionals. Ricky Davis and David Brcic both made the CONCACAF All-Star Team, firsts for U.S. players. Both are currently playing for the New York Cosmos. Tony Crudo became a solid defender and found a place with the Tampa Bay Rowdies, later with the California Surf, and presently with the Seattle Sounders. Gary Etherington later played for the New York Cosmos, then the San Jose Earthquakes.

After this first experience, it was necessary to set up a national program that would develop and screen our young talent. Staff and coaches were appointed, along with national and state administrators, to carry out a selection process so that in future Youth World Cups we would not have to refer to paper or telephone selections.

The system was put into full gear by the Youth Selection Committee, and it soon began functioning at about 80 percent efficiency. The politics, for the most part, were left out, since decisions for selecting the final pool of players came from regional staff coaches. There was always some pressure on these coaches, but few, if any, were ever influenced. With the selection process more accurate, the project was to provide the National Youth Team with more and more international play. Games were organized with European

opposition and, when financially feasible, a group of young, potential National Youth Team players was sent abroad.

The ongoing process of exposing and developing players began to pay some dividends. The players would, from now on, be chosen on the basis of their performance on the field. The decisions would no longer be made only on paper.

The team assembled in Tampa, Florida, to train for eight days prior to departure for Honduras. The University of South Florida, through soccer coach Dan Holcomb, made its training field available to the team, when it was not being used by the Tampa Bay Rowdies. Practices included two-a-days, at 9:30 and 4:30. The team had several scrimmages with the Rowdies, who were in their off season, and an all-important scrimmage against the Haitian All-Stars from Miami. It was obvious that goals would be hard to come by, especially with the Bowan brothers missing—two very important front runners. The whole team was built around an experienced Perry Van Der Beck at midfield. The plan was then to attack with one and one-half forwards—Mark Peterson playing in the center and John Hayes on the wing. (Perry was the first American ever to score a goal in international competition in Western Europe while on a national team. He scored on a free kick against West Germany's National Youth Team in 1977 during the Monaco Tournament of eight nations. It was a historic moment for the U.S. soccer—it had taken us over fifty years to accomplish just one goal.)

Upon arrival in Honduras, the team

was met by television crews and large crowds. We received a police escort to the seminary, and along the way thousands of people lined the dirt roads, welcoming the U.S. team to Tegucigalpa.

We trained twice a day for six days on the soccer field at the Catholic Seminary where we were being housed. We shared the field with the Canadians, who had arrived some ten days earlier. To call the training ground a soccer field was a euphemism. The field was covered with rocks, cinders, and cow manure. The goals were made from pipe that was falling apart, and the chicken wire nets successfully ruined eight of our soccer balls.

It was time to improvise. The pasture was 60 yards by 90 yards and was totally unplayable. We did exercises on an individual basis, with many minutes of 5 v. 2 and volley shooting on goal—if you cared to call it a goal.

Our opening game was against Puerto Rico, a team made up of the best players in Puerto Rico—regardless of age. They seemed to have forgotten some of their passports, or at least that was their official statement when the referees came around to inspect passports in an effort to verify ages. Most of the players had been in the lineup in San Juan, when the U.S. Olympic "B" Team played a series of three games there three months earlier.

The game went as expected, with the young Americans being a bit nervous and tentative, and the older disorganized Puerto Ricans defending with nine and playing very aggressively, bordering on rough. The instructions to the U.S. team members were to play to Van Der Beck, allowing him to scheme

the attacks. Jim Tiejens (Ft. Lauderdale Strikers) was solid in goal, and the defense was confident. Mark McKain (New Jersey Rockets) and Jeff Stock (Seattle Sounders) as wing backs, Jeff Durgan (New York Cosmos) stopping, and Sandje Ivanchukov (Tampa Bay) sweeping made a very formidable back four. In the midfield, it was Van Der Beck and Ray Vigliotti (Baltimore Blast). In the attack, it was John Hayes (St. Louis Steamers) and Mark Peterson, with Rick Marvin, a converted defender, as a withdrawn left winger.

In the middle of the first half, Ray Vigliotti hammered one home for the U.S. team, when he fired a shot into the upper ninety of the goal. This goal relaxed the team. Puerto Rico had difficulty breaking half-field, and Jim Tiejens remained untested. In the second half, only great saves by the Puerto Rican goalkeeper kept the score down. Rick Marvin finally rifled one from the left side from an acute angle to give the U.S. a 2–0 victory. It had been a good opener for the young Americans.

In the next game, the U.S. faced Trinidad, a very quick team with one-on-one, skillful players. But the result: a 4–0 U.S. victory. Perry Van Der Beck was the main force, scoring and assisting.

In retrospect, however, this game had been a factor in the U.S. team's failure to survive to the finals. Because of the odd alignment of the tournament, the U.S. faced Trinidad again—this time losing 3–1. This meant that wins were necessary over both Canada and Honduras if the U.S. was to survive. The second game against Trinidad had been a morning game. Breakfast was not served until 9 A.M., and kickoff was scheduled for 11. Steve Gay, our team manager, and Bill Muse, the assistant coach, did everything possible to provide juice and cereal as early before game time as they could.

Trinidad prepared well, marking Van Der Beck out of the game, with some physical marking by one of their "enforcers." John Hayes was hit early on the right thigh, bringing his speed down almost 50 percent. We knew we were in trouble. An early—and questionable—penalty kick didn't help the situation.

By the time we faced Canada, our backs were against the wall. The game was played in the evening in front of 32,000 spectators anxious to see the battle of the North Americans. The Canadian team looked very formidable with Chris Turner (San Diego Sockers) in goal, young Lenarduzzi (Vancouver Whitecaps) sweeping, Sweeney (Edmonton), Sagota (Ft. Lauderdale), and Nagy (Baltimore Blast) on the attack. It was an up-and-down battle from the starting whistle. Tiejens was brilliant in goal for the U.S. Durgan stopped Sagota, and Stock flanked Nagy. The final score was 0–0. The best chance of the evening came when Chris Turner (Canada) miskicked the ball and placed it on the foot of Mark Peterson. Peterson, in turn, chipped the ball over the empty Canadian goal.

In our next game, against Honduras, the U.S. would have to win by four goals to stay alive. This task was monumental, particularly against the still undefeated Hondurans, who were playing at home.

It was getting close to Christmas, and the rector of the seminary began playing Christmas carols at breakfast,

lunch, and dinner. This did not sit well with our players, who had now been away from home for some thirty days. Songs such as "I'll be home for Christmas" were all that was needed to take the players' concentration away from the big game.

The U.S. wanted to show some offense, but this can, naturally, only be done with an abundance of offensive players. The plan was, once gain, to free Van Der Beck and catch some goals on restart situations—particularly on corner kicks, where Durgan could outjump the Honduran defense. On paper this looked good. In practice, the plan didn't materialize. Honduras played quietly with possession of the ball, knowing that a tie or a loss by less than four goals would qualify them to the final four. The final result was a 1–0 victory for Honduras. They scored after time ran out—there was a bit of confusion between the referee and the scoreboard clock. At that point, we didn't care, for we had already been eliminated from the tournament. "I'll be home for Christmas" became a reality for the U.S. team.

Canada and Honduras made it from the Tegucigalpa group, while Costa Rica and Mexico qualified from the San Pedro Sula group. Canada traveled to San Pedro Sula to face Costa Rico and Mexico came to Tegucigalpa to challenge Honduras. Two winners from this final four would go on to Japan for the finals of the World Youth Cup. Honduras and Costa Rica appeared to be the favorites, but the predictions were all wrong. I suppose that as long as the soccer ball is round, it will be difficult to predict winners provided they are somewhat equally matched in talent. Canada demolished Costa Rica 4-0, and Mexico did a number on Honduras 2-0. It was unfortunate for Honduras. Their federation had worked hard to organize the tournament, and they were rather successful—especially when one considers what they had to work with. On the field, it had been a bitter disappointment. Canada and Mexico played in the final, although it held little significance as both were assured air tickets to Tokyo. Neither team showed spark. Canada, perhaps, had wanted this one a little more, only for psychological reasons. Nevertheless, Mexico was the victor in overtime 1-0.

But we were improving—especially when you consider that only four years of serious international play had passed. No time was lost in beginning preparations of our next youth team for qualification to the 1981 Youth World Cup to be played in Australia. Bob Gansler was hired as the second full-time coach for the USSF. His job was to assist me with the Senior World Cup team and to oversee the screening and selecting of the youth players. Later, he was appointed National Youth Coach.

The National Olympic Festival became a very important factor in screening and assessing top talent in America. Four regional teams—East, West, Midwest, and South—competed annually against each other to determine the best in the country. This type of competition was outstanding for our young players. They were able to stay away from home for a period of several weeks and live in a competitive environment, where they realized that every day counted if their performance was to take them to the National Team.

In July 1980 Bob and I chose the final twenty-two players for the U.S. National Youth Team, which was to compete in the CONCACAF qualifiers for the 1981 Australian finals. Choosing the first dozen or so players was not a difficult task. However, the quality of the next ten was not as pronounced, and the majority of the fifty or so players observed functioned at a similar level.

A game schedule was organized by Kurt Lamm for competition in Germany. Three of the games were played against senior amateur squads, one against a junior amateur team—all near Hanover, West Germany. The final part of the trip included participation in an international junior tournament hosted by the Hamburg State Federation at the Hamburg training center.

Craig Scarpelli looked to be the starter in goal, exhibiting talent, confidence, and maturity. The defense was not as clear. Billy McKeon, the captain, was certain, but whether he'd play stopper or sweeper was still to be determined. The wing backs were also unclear. Michael Menendez looked good, while Carl Bennett, Dave McMillan, and Eric Reice were working hard to win the other spot. Jay Ainslie was being flip-flopped from wing back to stopper. In the middle, Todd Saldana and John Stollmeyer were definites. The other spot was a mixture between Keith Meyer, Brian Fuerst, and Darryl Doran. In the attack, on the right side, Tom Kain looked dangerous. Steve McLean, Kevin Fouser, Tim Whitman, and Peter Skouras looked promising.

After an exhausting trip to Hanover the team needed two days rest. It rained every day. The training fields, because of the rain, are composed of red cinders,

not grass. It was not very beneficial for our players to train in flats on such a hard surface. At any rate, the competition was ideal. Against the amateur teams, we did well. This was a good indication that our youth team had some front runners and depth, unlike the squad that had played in Honduras. Victories of 2–0 and 7–0 and a 2–2 tie gave our players confidence.

The true test came against the European powers of Finland and Switzerland, along with the West German regional team. In this competition, we came out with a 3–1 win over Finland, a 2–1 loss to West Germany, and a 1–0 loss to Switzerland. We were unlucky with the two losses, for the U.S. had dominated both. But we were not discouraged, nor did we lose confidence.

The team returned to the U.S. for the qualifying round. Princeton University was the site to battle it out for a spot in the quarterfinals to be played at RFK Stadium in Washington, D.C. The other four nations at Princeton were El Salvador (their senior team later qualified for the World Cup in Spain), Antigua, Barbados, and the Netherland Antilles.

The American players, upon returning from Europe, received a seven-day break in their schedule and returned home for a little r. and r. Reassembling a week later, two more players were added to the roster. Darryl Gee (Cosmos) had not made the trip to Europe due to an ankle injury sustained during the Olympic Festival. The other player, David Lischner from Philadelphia, was highly recommended by several staff coaches, including Tom Smith and Rich Sheridan. He was

invited for a trial at Princeton and clinched a spot on the team within one day.

In the opening games, El Salvador was matched up against Antigua, while the U.S. played Barbados for the nightcap. It was a great feeling for the American players to see a very vocal and supportive American crowd cheer the U.S. team on. The small Princeton soccer stadium was an ideal site for the competition. The Princeton Athletic Department had done an excellent job making the natural grass turf as smooth as a carpet.

El Salvador had no difficulty in dealing with Antigua, blowing them away 7–0. In the U.S. game, our team started off tentatively, at least until the first goal was scored by Tom Kain. The rest was history as four more goals were scored by Fouser, Stollmeyer, Lischner, and Menendez. The team had played a disciplined game with confidence and had shown scoring potential.

On the second night of competition, the U.S. team played the Netherland Antilles and prevailed 3–0. The game was not as easy as the opener had been. The Antilles team had some quality players, although they lacked organizational sense. In this game, Fouser, Kain, and Gee were the goal getters. Billy McKeon policed the defense from the sweeper position, and Jay Ainslie did the stopping. Michael Menendez, from his rightback position, pushed forward into the attack at will and was involved in two goals.

Most of the almost 4,000 American fans present on the evening of August 7, 1980, saw with their own eyes where the expression "soccer war" comes from. Both the U.S. team and El Salvador were undefeated and unscored upon. There were already some ill feelings between the two squads, and some of the El Salvador players had tried taunting the young Americans into fisticuffs. The Americans showed enough class to stay away from fighting and waited patiently for the big game.

Both teams played with caution for the first twenty-five minutes, marking tightly. Then finally, Carl Bennett, from his left back position, went into the attack and slipped a penetrating pass to Tom Kain, who took it on the run to give the U.S. a one-goal lead. The score remained 1–0 until half-time. However, following Kain's goal, the El Salvador players began to look for trouble, taking cheap shots at the Americans, kicking from behind, spitting, and sucker punching whenever possible. The Cuban referee was scared and lost control of the game. A contingent of El Salvadorian immigrants from Trenton were there to cheer their team on. Their cheers were in vain, as a group of young American female tennis players, competing in a tournament also being played at Princeton, drowned out their every word.

At halftime, Coach Gansler and I reviewed tactics. Our key message was that El Salvador was sure to attempt to intimidate and bait our players, and it was imperative that we not retaliate. Sure enough, in the second half, Tom Kain was sucker punched by an El Salvadorian player directly in front of the scorekeeper's bench, the referee, and the disciplinary committee. Tom did not react, but took the punch as a man, holding his hands at his side.

Before the final whistle blew, John Stollmeyer also received a shot to the face, loosening five of his teeth. It was a bloody mess to say the least. He reacted, and both players were sent off. The disciplinary committee on the following day suspended one of El Salvador's players for a year and the coach for three years—he was suspended from coaching as well as playing.

Tom Kain went on to score his second goal to give the U.S. a 2–0 victory and a berth in the quarterfinals. On that evening, the American fans were in full support of their team, and the American flag flew high.

The fourth and final game was an exercise that had to be completed. The U.S., fielding a completely reserve squad, won easily over the weakest team in the tournament, Antigua, 3–1. It was the first goal given up by the U.S. team. Brian Fuerst (two) and Tim Whitman scored for the U.S.

Tom Kain was voted the MVP for the Princeton venue. With four goals, he was the leading scorer and had played extremely well on the field. It was another first for America as a U.S. player was voted MVP for an international tournament.

Mexico prevailed in the Los Angeles competition. Honduras won the SIU group, and Canada was at the top in the Texas group. There had been problems in those groups as well. Puerto Rico brought a team that was totally over age. They were sent home. Honduras had at least ten overaged players, of which three were sent home. Texas was unbearable because of the extremely high temperatures, leading to complaints from all the teams competing there.

In the Washington quarterfinal

competition, Honduras and Bermuda advanced from the Edwardsville group, while the U.S. and the Netherland Antilles made it from the Princeton site. El Salvador had been eliminated. Honduras played the Netherland Antilles, the second place entry from Princeton, while the U.S. matched up against Bermuda, the second place team from the Illinois site. The Netherland Antilles scored first against Honduras in the opening of the doubleheader at RFK. However, the Honduras team was too skillful and experienced, and calmly walked away with a 9–2 victory.

The U.S. game against Bermuda was a sleeper. The U.S. team was lethargic, and the Bermuda players were cautious, creating little excitement for the duration of the ninety minutes. David Lischner was taken down in the penalty box, and John Stollmeyer had no trouble scoring from the penalty spot. In the second half, Kevin Fouser scored from close range to give the U.S. a 2–0 lead. However, Bermuda fought back, and a faulty pass by Carl Bennett was intercepted by the Bermuda winger who went in one-on-one against Craig Scarpelli for a score. The U.S. survived in a very sluggish game 2–1.

The semifinals matched up Mexico against Canada and the U.S. against Honduras. The experts predicted Mexico and Honduras would win and go on to be represented in Australia. Half of their prediction was accurate.

Heavy rains saturated the RFK Stadium before the kickoff of the doubleheader. The ball on a ground pass would travel no more than five yards. It was almost impossible to play. However, the games had to be completed with the two winners

determined that Friday, August 15.

The conditions took much away from the Mexicans' skillful style, giving the advantage to Canada, whose style is much more direct with air attacking tactics. Mexico scored first, before the field had a chance to go totally underwater. However, they could not hold the lead, and Canada equalized before halftime. The second half was a game of "who can kick the ball out of the puddle." The game ended in a tie, as did the two overtime periods. Mexico finally succeeded in taking the game on penalty kicks, 4-3. They had earned their tickets to Australia.

For the nightcap, conditions worsened, and between the mud and the puddles, it was difficult to do anything that resembled soccer. Both teams were testing different ways of moving the ball. However, neither team could find a solution. The Americans, for the most part, went over the top, sending long air balls from the back hoping to reach Lischner, Kain, or Fouser. Honduras had difficulty sending long passes, since their style calls for short passes—almost to the degree of "overpassing." They couldn't combine anything and hardly looked dangerous. The U.S. team's tight marking didn't help their situation.

Finally, in the second half, Tom Kain ran on a diagonal and received a through pass from David Lischner inside the penalty box. The Honduran goalie came out, but was unsuccessful in his attempt to block the shot. Kain slipped the ball by him toward the empty net. The ball traveled slowly, and the Honduran left back came diving in from the left and deflected the ball wide with his hand. John Stollmeyer hammered the ball into the upper corner on the penalty kick, giving the U.S. a 1–0 lead. It looked good for the U.S. until the final minutes of the game. Michael Menendez was kicked in the head from the blind side, temporarily losing consciousness. After treatment from trainer Don Kessler, he was revived, although still dazed.

We moved him into the attack and brought back Tom Kain as a defender. With little time remaining, a corner kick was awarded to Honduras. Moments earlier, Steve McLean had sent a beautiful header toward the ninety area of the goal. However, a great save by the Honduran goalie prevented Steve from locking up the game. Menendez, now claiming to feel better, switched back to the defense. As the switch was made, a Honduran player, coming from the blind side of Menendez, timed a good corner kick serve to equalize. The U.S. team was deflated. Two fifteen-minute overtimes didn't settle the score, so a repeat performance of the first game of the evening followed. Penalty kicks would decide the finalist and would earn one of the teams the right to go to Australia—not a very good way of breaking a tie, but then rules are rules.

Each country nominated five players to take the twelve-yard kicks, alternating kicks against the opponent's goalie until a winner was established. If the first five kicks ended in a tie, kicks would continue on a sudden death basis, providing both teams had an equal number of kicks.

It was a nerve-wracking situation. Six thousand strong American supporters stayed until the bitter end to cheer the U.S. youth squad. Drama set in after both teams were tied at six each,

then seven, and then eight. The ninth shooter for the U.S., Kevin Fouser, scored, and Craig Scarpelli became the hero as he deflected the opponent's kick, ending the ordeal. It was a very courageous way in which to earn a spot, for the first time in U.S. history, among the final sixteen. The Washington fans were simply fantastic. (It was reported, however, that some of our national soccer "leaders" were cheering for the other team—a sad commentary on U.S. soccer.) The celebration was on—champagne corks were popping in the U.S. locker room. Unfortunately, the bus that was to bring the team back to the American University dorm left early—without the team. However, the mood was such that the two-hour wait outside RFK didn't bother anyone in the least. What had mattered was qualifying.

Saturday was a travel day for the team, now on its way to Giants Stadium at the Meadowlands for the final to determine the CONCACAF champion. It was billed as a doubleheader with the Cosmos v. the Washington Diplomats game being the second of the evening.

It was difficult to bring the players up for the last one—they were emotionally and physically drained. They had left everything in the nation's capital. The game was sluggish and unexciting. The AstroTurf didn't help our players. The Mexicans too hardly showed any enthusiasm. It appeared that both teams just wanted to go home. It was almost three months now that the U.S. players had been away from home. Mexico scored in each of the halves to give them the CONCACAF trophy for the third time in a row.

The U.S. team departed the next day

for home, with instructions that they had but one year to prepare themselves for Australia. Specific soccer training methods were discussed with the players, and each player received an analysis of his strengths and weaknesses. Improvement in skill tactical awareness had been the major problems for the U.S. team.

The Road to Australia

The U.S. would face some of the finest young soccer players in the world in Australia—many of whom were on the threshold of becoming international stars for their respective countries. In the 1977 championship games in Tunisia, several superstars emerged. "Junior" of Brazil was the favorite of the fans, as well as Oleh Taran of the Soviet Union. In the 1979 World Youth Cup, a number of young players became overnight successes because of their outstanding performances before and during the competition. The most heralded of them all was Diego Maradona of Argentina. His marked value at the present time is in the millions. He has been labeled as the new Pele.

The standard of play exhibited at this level compares with the highest professional standards. It is quite understandable when you consider that many of the players are members of clubs from the top soccer leagues of their respective countries. The players in the Australian tournament would have a higher marked value than had ever been seen before in previous tournaments. Their combined worth would easily run into the millions.

Maradona, who was reportedly sold

for $8 million, became a member of the senior National Team immediately following his outstanding performance in the 1979 World Youth Cup. Similarly, it is expected that many of the youth players who participated in Australia will also move up to the senior squads. Steven Blair of the Australia National Youth Team became a member of their senior squad even before the Youth Championship in Australia. Ricky Davis of the U.S. joined the senior team immediately following his performance in the Youth World Cup qualifying round in Puerto Rico.

The 1981 youth tournament quickly became very prestigious due to the keen interest on the part of the Europeans who were making a serious attempt to produce winning teams. After Argentina's double in the World Cup and the World Youth Championship in 1978 and 1979, the Europeans wanted desperately to prove that they were capable of the same.

The European youth tournament to decide the six qualifiers for Australia had been completed six months earlier. The six finalists, in order, were: England—the winners of the tournament, Poland, Italy, Spain, Romania, and West Germany. The West German team was a late substitute for Holland. Holland had actually qualified but decided to withdraw from further participation due to domestic difficulties with clubs and player releases. England, which had almost ignored the two previous youth competitions, wanted to restore its international reputation. This youth tournament would be a good place to begin. The English team was comprised of young players from first-division teams, including the likes of Paul Allen from West Ham, who had already played in the F.A. Cup final at Wembley.

Poland was the other team favored from Europe. They looked very formidable in the European tournament and were unlucky in their runnerup finish. West Germany would be an unknown in the final round, since their coach, Dietrich Weise, removed all the young Bundesliga players and brought in a younger, less experienced team. Nevertheless, it was a team that wanted to win. Weisze had been disappointed with the performance of the team represented in the European tournament and consequently made wholesale changes. As we will see, the changes paid off.

From the South American countries, the three perennial qualifiers were there again. Brazil, always consistent, would try to win this one with many first-division, experienced players, who exhibited a very exciting soccer style with a collection of one-on-one players in their lineup. Uruguay, whose senior national squad won the Gold Cup the previous January, was the best in the South American tournament. They brought with them a rich tradition of World Cup participation and three players whose dollar value was well over $1 million. Villazan, the midfielder from Nacional, and Francescoli, the front runner, were unstoppable in the qualifying round. Argentina had reached the final sixteen as well, but without the services of Maradona or Diaz the task had not been quite as easy. Additionally, Coach Magnotti had decided not to take the youth team this time around.

Some of the other nations showing potential in Australia included Cameroon, Egypt, and the disciplined South Korean team, which had looked very strong in the qualifying games. Korea had beaten Qatar 4–1 under the brilliant leadership of team captain Choi-Soon-Ho.

Arrangements for international play for our team were made whenever possible. Holiday breaks such as Christmas and Easter proved to be the most convenient times as far as player availability. The first of such competitions was played in Brazil in January 1981. The team trained for seven days in Tampa, Florida. After several scrimmages against the Tampa Bay Rowdies, the Olympic Developmental team, and a Bayern Regional Senior Amateur Select Team, the youth team left semiprepared. Bob Gansler and Jay Miller were the coaches for the Brazil tournament.

It was apparent already in Tampa, and later in Brazil, that most of the players had lost form since the summer competition. College and high-school competition was not sufficient to sustain, much less improve, the players' level of play. It was particularly the front runners who lost their timing and individual rhythm and their ability to play under higher-paced match conditions. Playing against Brazil in the opening match, the U.S. team ran out of energy, giving up four goals in the second half. Against Uruguay, the team had looked competitive in the back and middle thirds of the field. However, the finishing third was nonexistent. The U.S. went down for the second time 2–0. In their last game, against Bolivia, the team began to jell and looked to be the winner when David Lischner scored from a pass belonging to Al Smith. However, a penalty kick and an offside goal gave Bolivia a 2-1 victory. The tournament gave us an idea of what had to be done in the months to come. It also served to test some new players, of which Chris Hundelt, Al Smith, and Tom Gardiner looked good enough to make the final roster. Chris Hundelt was sweeping for the injured Billy McKeon, and Tom Gardiner looked good as a stopper.

The players were given an analysis of their performance and left for home to work on their game. The unfortunate part of working with the U.S. teams lies in the fact that the coaches see the players for two or three weeks at a time, with long intervals between the weeks of training. It is very difficult to check on the players' improvement and to continue them at a high level of training.

The next stage of preparation for the team occurred in April when the team, with only players born in 1962 or later, participated in the Bellinzona, Switzerland, tournament. The U.S. team trained in Florence, Italy, in a beautiful Italian Federation training center. Training sites of this type are all over Europe, something that the U.S. is in dire need of. The eight-day stay helped in preparing the team physically. Several scrimmages against local opposition aided the team in an organizational sense. The bus trip to Bellinzona took over seven hours with intermittent stops, a very scenic trip for the young Americans.

The U.S. team was well liked and accepted by the general public in Bellinzona. On two other occasions, the U.S. team had participated in this tournament. On the first occasion, the U.S. won the competition, defeating Tunisia in the final, blanking all the other teams along the way. David Brcic was in goal, and Ricky Davis, Gary Etherington, and Don Ebert did all the scoring. The following year a whole new team arrived to defend the title but fell short, losing to Milano in the final game 1–0. Nevertheless, the U.S. had taken the first three games. The fans knew we could play and looked forward to seeing us perform.

After a year of absence from the tournament, the U.S. team's first game was against the local pro club's youth team, which resulted in a draw. It was a bit disappointing for the team, although the overall level of play was good. In its second game, the U.S. team defeated Nuremberg of West Germany 2–1. It was in this game that Tom Kain began to regain his playing form. The next game for the U.S. was against Fiorantina of Italy. Unfortunately, the Americans could only come up with a scoreless tie. It was very difficult for the U.S. team to break the Italian bunker, although Lischner and Jianette did both have chances to score. Playing again, this time against another Italian club team, Napoli, the U.S. players ran into the same problem of trying to break the solid Italian defense.

The team this time finished fourth out of the eight participating club and national teams. The coaching staff was pleased with the team's performance, knowing that key players such as McKeon, Scarpelli, Gee, Meyer, and Ainslie would be waiting to reinforce the team in Mexico for a June tournament. Al Smith, Tom Gardiner, and Chris Hundelt had succeeded in solidifying their positions on the final team during the Bellinzona competition. Early in June 1981, the team assembled in Colorado Springs at the Olympic Training Center to prepare for the Dr. Havelange Youth Tournament, which was hosted by the Mexican Federation. Seven nations, plus the host country, participated. The U.S., Brazil, Spain, and Mexico were playing in Mexico City at Azteca Stadium. Paraguay, Yugoslavia, Poland, and Argentina were housed in Monterey. My resignation as coach of the National and National Youth Teams, submitted a month earlier, was to become effective in mid-October 1981, after the Youth World Cup finals.

We opened against Mexico on a rainy night, this time playing better than we had the year before at the Meadowlands. The mud didn't help our game, and two faulty passes by Ainslie and Hundelt gave Mexico a 2–0 halftime lead. The U.S. came storming back in the second half. Tom Kain put the game within reach on a fine goal scored from a Stollmeyer pass. Time ran out as Jianette and Gee missed equalizing chances.

The second game against Brazil was played at the site where the two countries were being housed. The field was heavy (it was the rainy season in Mexico), and the American players had slowly begun to develop that famous dysentery problem, and diarrhea and vomiting became part of the program. Several players were scratched from the lineup against Brazil because of the health problem. Brazil came out thinking that the game would be a repeat performance of six months ago.

On this day, the Americans would make life more difficult.

The U.S. team played even, if not outplaying, the powerful Brazilian side. But the end result was a 1–0 Brazilian victory, the single goal scored when a free kick squirted out from under Scarpelli's stomach as he lay in the mud. Despite the loss, it was a positive result for the U.S. team psychologically. They had played against the best and were very much in the game.

The last game, against Spain, was again a trip to Azteca Stadium. It was getting difficult to field eleven players now. Of the eighteen players that had made the trip, fourteen spent most of the day in the bathroom. Dehydration had set in, and most of the players were extremely weak. Needless to say, we were never in the game against Spain but fought hard in an effort to save face. It was 2–0 until the last few minutes, when Spain intercepted a pass in our back third to bring the score to 3–0.

The entire delegation was ecstatic when the fourth game against Poland was cancelled. Poland and the other European countries had problems very similar to ours.

It was in July at the Olympic Festival that the Youth Team acted as a sparring partner for the four regional under-23 teams. In this competition, two new players were added to the youth team roster—George Fernandez from the University of California at Hayward and Mark Devey from Bethlehem, Pennsylvania. The only sad note in the sparring matches at the festival was that Billy McKeon, the skipper, incurred a serious knee injury that eventually would put him out of the final competition. This was an important loss

And victory is sweet!

for the U.S. team. Darryl Gee sustained a quadricep pull, making him questionable for the Australian trip. Michael Menendez' ankle showed little improvement, also putting him on the doubtful list.

In late August, the USSF reciprocated and hosted an international tournament in Colorado Springs. For this tournament, Mexico, Canada, and Bermuda were invited. Both Canada and Bermuda brought older players to prepare them for the next Olympics. These two teams had already been eliminated from Youth World Cup play.

In a round-robin tournament, the U.S. team came in second place to none other than Mexico, losing to them 1-0. This time, the team was right on par with Mexico. However, a great goal by Tom Kain was disallowed when the referee failed to apply the advantage rule. A victory over Canada 3-0 and a come-from-behind draw with Bermuda gave confidence to the U.S. squad.

After the last game of the tournament in Colorado Springs, a meeting was held to discuss the departure for Germany, then Australia. Equipment, travel itinerary for the entire tour, and the possibility of playing in the People's Republic of China were all covered. For the most part, it was a constructive meeting, with one exception. One of our federation leaders made a statement to this effect: "Boys, I know we don't really belong in the final competition, but at least we are going to look spic and span, with shoes polished." To this day, every player in that room remembers the words. Their confidence was deflated—the players simply did not want to be associated with the leaders.

When we departed New York, Harry Weise, the equipment manager, had enough equipment to dress the team for a year. For the first time, the team looked first class in travel dress. The trip to Germany, again via Amsterdam, was a long one. We were bused from Amsterdam to the Duisberg Training Center for ten days of training, which included three practice matches against very formidable opposition. The training center in Duisberg was first class, the food excellent, and the fields were manicured like a putting green. We had excellent preparation for the team. They played some very inspired soccer, winning over the West German Regional team 2-1, and then upsetting a second division Bundesliga senior team, Bayer 05 Schwartz Essen, 2-0. In the next game, the U.S. lost 2-1 to the Bayer 05 Rot Essen. This team was a first-division Bundesliga team, and many of the players had been seen by the Americans on educational television's "Soccer Made in Germany." Keith Meyer had the greatest thrill of his life as he matched up against Dieter Hertzog, a great international for Germany. Hertzog played on the German National Team when they won the World Cup in 1974.

Darryl Gee joined the team in Duisberg a week later, with his quadricep muscle working at 75 percent. Darryl Doran agreed to join the team in Amsterdam the day the team was scheduled to leave for Australia. Billy McKeon was uncertain about his injury, about his schooling, and about his playing with St. Louis University. He chose not to come.

The flight on KLM airlines, departing from Amsterdam, took thirty-seven hours. It was long and tiring, but everyone persevered and survived. Coca Cola U.S.A. had decided to put the team up for an additional seven days of training on the Gold Coast, outside of Brisbane. The vacation resort, a twin of Ft. Lauderdale only smaller, was heaven. John Bevilaqua, the Coca Cola representative, had made arrangements for the team to stay in plush condominiums for the seven-day duration.

It was a very relaxing atmosphere, and the people of Australia were very congenial. We trained twice a day, once in the morning and then again under the lights at a time close to when our games were scheduled for. During the seven days, the team had one scrimmage against a pro team from the Queensland Regional League and won 3–0. John Stollmeyer was in top form, scoring all three goals for the U.S.

The team then moved on to Brisbane, where we were housed with the three other countries that formed our group—Poland, Qatar, and Uruguay. The hotel and food were first class. However, the atmosphere created by serving meals to all the teams at the same time in the same dining room made everyone uneasy. Qatar, the Arabian representative in the tournament, had its own chef, who prepared a special diet. (They also brought tons of money.)

The rugby and cricket stadium where the games were to be played was playable, although certainly not the fields the players had fallen in love with in Germany. The midfield was torn up by rugby cleats, and was unplayable for one-touch combination passes. The opening of the first round had Poland

playing Qatar and the U.S. against Uruguay. The favorites, naturally, were Poland, as the second best team from Europe, and Uruguay, the best team from South America.

Half wrong again, as Qatar upset Poland 1–0, despite having only two shots on goal. The lone goal was scored by accident. The Polish sweeper, from outside his penalty area, tried to clear the ball. On rushed the Qatar center forward. The ball struck him directly on the knee, rebounding at 80 m.p.h. into the upper corner of the Polish goal.

Was it planned or was it luck? That was the question posed by the 18,000 spectators (maybe even the Qatar team). This team seemed to have caught much of the same luck throughout the tournament. Poland was stunned by the goal and could not endure the Qatar "miracle." They lost all confidence after four breakaways were missed by the Polish forwards. Qatar gained two points plus a $25,000 bonus to each player.

In the second game, the U.S. was charged up to do the same to the favorite, Uruguay. From the whistle, the Latins came charging, using all the cylinders to get on the scoreboard. They did, in the seventh minute, when the expensive young star from club champions Nacional took the ball on the U.S. thirty-yard line and danced through four Americans before slipping a pass to Villazan for the first score. The nervous U.S. team was still finding and feeling its way and played very precariously.

Finally, John Stollmeyer began to win many one-on-one duels at midfield. This inspired the American squad, and they began to move into the attack. The last twenty minutes belonged to the U.S. Several near misses by Kain and Gee, and a thirty-yard bomb by Stollmeyer negated by the Latin goalkeeper, kept the U.S. from scoring by the end of the half.

At halftime, we made several minor adjustments and felt that Kain could free himself from the left back of Uruguay. From the second half kickoff, the U.S. pressed. In the fifty-sixth minute, Tom Kain freed himself deep in the corner on the left side of the field. He dribbled toward the Uruguay goal, drawing its sweeper out of the middle. He then slipped a perfect pass to Darryl Gee on the seven-yard line. Gee and the goalie were face-to-face. Any shot to the left or right of the goalie, and the game would have been tied. Gee hit the goalie.

Twenty-five minutes into the second half, a blatant offside goal by Uruguay gave them a 2–0 lead. This deflated the U.S. squad. With minutes on the clock, Uruguay scored its third and best of the evening, when Francescoli hammered one into the upper ninety, over the outstretched hands of Craig Scarpelli. It was as good a performance by the U.S. team as one expected. With a bit of luck, borrowed from Qatar, the U.S. team would have made history.

The second round of games was critical for the losers. If they were to lose again, their chances of advancing to the next round would be nil. Uruguay opened against Poland, and completely outplayed the demoralized Polish squad. However, they could only produce one goal.

In the second game, the U.S. v. Qatar, we played with more confidence, pressed hard, and controlled the game.

Finally, Mark Devey made history as the first American to score a goal for the U.S. in Youth World Cup competition. He took a fine pass from David Lischner after the U.S. team beat Qatar's frequently used offside trap tactic and raced in one-on-one with the Qatar goalie. With poise, he parked the ball in the far corner of the opponent's goal.

After the intermission, Qatar, knowing that a $25,000 bonus check was at stake, began to bite, but not for long. The U.S. defense, policed by Tom Gardiner and Co., gave the opposition no chances. It looked clear for the U.S. victory.

With little time remaining, a ball was crossed from the left by a Qatar player, around the U.S. eight-yard line. Tom Gardiner barely touched the ball with his head. The Qatar center forward raced in to strike on goal. He headed the ball to the near post. Craig Scarpelli went to his left and pushed the ball wide by the post. Another Qatar player raced in and struck the ball over the U.S. crossbar. Both Qatar players were holding their heads in despair, wanting to hide. While this was going on, a dwarfed linesman from Ethiopia raised his flag indicating a goal. He claimed that on the initial header, the ball crossed over the goal line. The chief referee accepted his decision and allowed the goal to stand. After an evening of protesting by the U.S. delegation, followed by video tape viewing in the Brisbane studio (which clearly illustrated, in slow motion, that there was no goal and that the ball never crossed over the goal line), the score stood 1–1.

It is a sad moment for all in soccer when a bad decision by some unknown invited to referee in a World Cup is allowed to stand. The fact is that if the sixteen best teams in the world are brought together, then the sixteen best referees in the world should be brought together as well. It cannot be political, i.e., inviting referees from every corner of the world to please their countries' federations. That single decision had cost the United States Soccer Federation over $500,000 in preparation expenses, plus all the years put in by the soccer volunteers in America, who had hoped to help make the U.S. a competitive side.

With Uruguay gaining four points, they were through to the next round. Qatar, now with three points (and three shots on goal), needed only to lose by less than three goals to advance. They lost 1–0. Even in this game, the dwarfed Ethiopian referee awarded a penalty to Qatar, while being positioned at half-field. Qatar missed the penalty. Uruguay played without its four superstars—they knew the game didn't matter.

There was only one chance for the U.S. team—they would have to beat Poland by four goals. This kind of miracle against the second best team in Europe was but a dream. In contrast, it was Poland that actually won the game by four goals, tearing the injured and demoralized Americans apart. Poland had to save face. It was their best performance by far. John Stollmeyer, David Lischner, and Darryl Gee were out. The injured Tom Gardiner, limping with a swollen knee, still played bravely, but could not stop the Polish raids on the American goal.

The first appearance of the U.S. team in the Youth World Cup had been

something to be proud of. Some "experts" had unrealistic expectations of the U.S. squad to do well in the finals. Those that knew realized that the U.S. team would have to play up to its fullest potential to have any success at all. These young Americans had opened the door to participation in the World Cup—this was a beginning. Every great soccer nation started the same way. Phase two would be to win a game in the final round. They had come close, getting a tie and scoring a historic goal. A bright picture lies ahead for U.S. soccer, provided soccer is managed by qualified people.

Uruguay and Qatar advanced to the next round. Many experts believed that Uruguay was the team to beat in the competition. They played as a solid, cohesive unit. They had experience and tradition on their side. Their senior squad had been in almost every World Cup competition, and the youth team had made it to the final round of the previous two World Youth Championships.

Qatar was the team that surprised all. As they qualified through, they seemed to gain more energy and confidence. With each win their players and coaches also became richer. They would receive $50,000 per player in the next round. Qatar's Shah, a soccer fanatic, had sent the team to the competition in a private jet. Money was no obstacle, as they offered the Uruguay Youth Team $100,000 to play an exhibition in Qatar. They also wanted to buy two of the Uruguayan players at $250,000 each.

Another problem had arisen in Sydney, one that had to be resolved then and there. As in the past two experiences with the U.S. Senior Team, the inevitable happened as the youth players discussed the possibility of not going on to China—in other words, it was strike time. Their reasons and requests were valid, and we, as coaches, along with John Bevilaqua of Coca Cola, had to resolve it. It had been a long and demanding experience for the young players, emotionally, physically, and financially. They had the ability to overcome the emotional and physical demands placed on them, but financially they were unable to survive. They were broke. Jay Ainslie, the captain, on the evening prior to my departure for the States, approached Gansler, Bevilaqua, and me with the players' problem. After two previous experiences as a strike mediator, I had no difficulty in dealing with this one. Looking over all the options, it was apparent that, without money, the China tour would be a headache to all concerned. The players would not be able to purchase any souvenirs—or Chinese tea for that matter. John Bevilaqua agreed to approach his company for a per diem for each player, while Gansler and I were to approach Gene Edwards. In the end, both parties came through, and a per diem was agreed upon for the remainder of the tour. On October 14, as I was leaving for Philadelphia, Bob Gansler remarked to me how on my last day as National Coach, "the player strike is still haunting you." I had learned how to settle strikes.

The team left for China with fifteen semihealthy players, while Gee, Stollmeyer, and Doran returned home. John Stollmeyer, voted as one of the top three midfielders in the Brisbane group,

was hospitalized with appendicitis. Bob Gansler took the team, as my resignation was effective as of October 15, 1981. I returned to Philadelphia to take the coaching responsibility for the Philadelphia Fever, a member of the Major Indoor Soccer League.

The team went on to compete in a four-nation tournament in the People's Republic of China. The other invited countries were Egypt and Australia. There had been concern on the part of Coca Cola, official sponsors of the event, as to whether Egypt would participate following the assassination of President Anwar Sadat. They did, however, continue to play.

The U.S. team survived the competition well, despite all the injuries that plagued the team. A mild upset over Australia, 2–1, gave the team new life. But losses to China and Egypt didn't help to further the on-field situation.

They had played well enough against Egypt to win, but again "fate" turned against them. In the China game, it was the Chinese senior team playing against the injury-riddled Americans, resulting in a 5–0 final result. Why China was ever permitted to play their senior squad is a mystery to all of us.

According to reports and remarks made by players upon their return from China, the educational and social experience, coupled with the soccer playing, was a chance of a lifetime. The players knew that few, if any, would ever touch that part of the world again.

World Youth Cup Finals—A Closer Look

The World Youth Championship for the Coca Cola Cup was the dream and realization of Dr. Joao Havelange, president of FIFA. Dr. Havelange had promised the world soccer community that he would do everything within his power to encourage the growth of soccer in underdeveloped countries. He put forward several projects, one of which was the World Youth Championship. No one realized just how quickly this tournament would become a success.

The first Youth World Cup in Tunisia attracted immediate attention and from there the success skyrocketed. The estimated viewing audience, both on site and by satellite, for the 1979 Youth World Cup in Japan was over 100 million. The potential audience for Australia was estimated at one billion.

All eyes were on the Tunisia tournament to see if FIFA, Coca Cola, and the Tunisian Federation could pull it off, both on and off the field. It was a complete success. The sixteen nations participating played a high standard of soccer, with the games becoming more and more emotional as the survivors closed in on the big final. Two exciting and emotionally draining semifinals were determined on penalty kicks, with Mexico beating Brazil 5–3 and the USSR defeating Uruguay 4–3. The final, played in Olympic Stadium in Tunis, was again decided on penalty kicks, with the Soviet Union prevailing over Mexico 9–8 after maintaining a 2–2 tie in regulation and overtime play.

The championship game was one that brought two countries with contrasting styles of play to the same field. It was the Soviet Union that was very methodical and, to a degree, stereotyped, as they looked to free their center forward Oleh Teran. Their basic attack was to build up in the middle and

then send penetrating passes to Teran or to free the wingers who in turn would go for the touchline and serve the ball into the penalty area.

On the other hand, the Mexicans played with longer possession time of the ball, both as individuals and as a team. Their raids on the Soviet Union goal were not as frequent, for their style and pace was much slower. Almost religiously, every Mexican player puts three or four touches on the ball before passing to a teammate. Occasionally, there were individuals who possessed a particular flair, but for the most part, very few of their players would reach world class.

The victory for the Soviet Union was a very important one for them. It helped them to regain some of the credibility lost over the past years as a result of their failure to qualify for the World Cup. This victory marked the rebuilding of their national teams. It paid off for them, as their senior team, four years later, qualified for Spain.

The second World Youth Championship, again sponsored by Coca Cola, had a different format in that no nation was invited to Japan. All countries had to qualify through a tough a grinding elimination series to reach the final sixteen. Ninety-six countries entered the qualifying competition, which gave the tournament the status of a major international event, giving the youth from all corners of the world the opportunity to exhibit their skills and national styles.

There were many surprises in the early round. Mexico was eliminated early before the quarterfinals, while Paraguay, featuring future Cosmos stars Romero and Cabanas, pushed the favored Russians in the quarterfinals, only to lose on penalty kicks. The semifinals matched Eastern European rivals Poland and the Soviet Union, and Latin American opponents Uruguay and Argentina, assuring a classic confrontation of European v. South American styles of play in the final.

Poland played well in a 1–0 losing effort to the Soviet Union. It was a bit of bad luck for Poland, as they had much of the game. However, the Soviet Union's experience of being there before became an overriding factor in their victory.

Argentina, under Coach Menotti, downed Uruguay 2–0. It was the play of Diaz and Maradona that captured the eyes of the entire soccer community. Diaz twice scored hat tricks and finished with eight goals, a high in the tournament. Maradona scored six goals and was named MVP, his first step in establishing international acclaim. The Argentinians demonstrated to the world what attacking soccer is all about.

The 1979 Japan tournament was a complete success. Held in Tokyo, Ohimiya, Yokohama, and Kobe, the ten-day tournament attracted over 300,000 spectators, including 52,000 for the final in Tokyo between Argentina and the Soviet Union. Gone were any lingering doubts about the future of the Coca Cola Cup. Dr. Havelange's dream had become a very successful reality.

Ninety-nine nations entered the competition for the 1981 Youth Cup in Australia, with a worldwide series of qualifying and elimination games to decide the fifteen nations that would join the host, Australia, for the October 3-18 finals. Qualifications were held in six regions—Africa, Asia, Europe,

CONCACAF, South America, and Oceania.

Each of the regions were assured a various number of berths, with the following teams earning the right to be among the final sixteen: Africa: Egypt and Cameroon; Asia: South Korea and Qatar; Europe: England, Poland, Italy, Spain, Romania, and West Germany; CONCACAF: Mexico and the United States; South America: Brazil and Uruguay; and Oceania: Argentina (the winner of an intercontinental playoff with New Zealand and Israel).

Six venues were used for the finals—Sydney, Melbourne, Brisbane, Adelaide, Newcastle, and Canberra. The opening ceremonies were held in Melbourne, while the closing ceremonies and final game were held in Sydney. The elimination series concluded on October 8. The winners and runnerups from each group restarted play in the quarterfinals on Sunday, October 11. In each case, the winner of one group would play the runnerup of another group.

Group A	Group B
Uruguay	Italy
Poland	Korea
Qatar	Romania
USA	Brazil

Group C	Group D
Spain	England
Egypt	Cameroon
Germany	Australia
Mexico	Argentina

From Group A, it was Uruguay that showed itself capable of being the champion. However, the Eastern

European Romania, disciplined and, to a degree, programmed, scored on two free kicks to give the Romanians a mild upset, 2–1. Germany gained momentum as the tournament progressed, and the young Germans were convinced by their play that they would be in the thick of the competition. They disposed of Australia in a rough match, 1–0. Australia was a bit unlucky; the German goalkeeper made several unbelievable saves in the dying moments. The Cinderella team, Qatar, again did the unusual, defeating Brazil 3–2. Brazil had the tournament officials check the passports of the Qatar players, but their appeal didn't stand. The game was played, and Qatar gained the victory on a penalty kick in the last minutes of the game. A Brazilian official was so upset at the penalty decision that he raced onto the field to protest the call to the Mexican referee. He failed. Qatar advanced to the semifinals.

Egypt opened up a 2–0 lead over England early in their game. In the second half, England pressured Egypt, found the going easy, and advanced to the semifinals on a 4–2 win.

Germany had experience playing the Eastern European neighbors and created an accurate tactical plan. They eliminated Romania to advance to the final. England, on the other hand, could not cope with Qatar's offside trap. It was difficult for the young English players to adjust to the trap, and the rhythm of the English attack was never consistent. Qatar won 2–1.

The final matched up West Germany and Qatar. There was much curiosity as to whether the Arab nation would continue to destroy the world soccer

powers. None of the experts wanted to commit themselves. Qatar had already proven them wrong on three different occasions. But Germany was confident. One gets the feeling that tradition and competition of great soccer powers are almost automatically filtered down to their rising young stars. Whether by the mere fact that these young players train with World Cup players in their respective clubs or by osmosis, the young talent learns and matures very quickly. West Germany proved that it could be done. They had brought in all new players—players with talent but little experience. They had learned quickly, and the combination of their will to win coupled with the gained experience made them unbeatable. They all knew that interesting contracts would be offered to them if they won the final. Qatar was to receive a huge bonus per player. They had already spent over $10 million on team preparation, and now they were willing to go for the works.

The big final in Sydney, on October 18 at 3:00 P.M., proved to be only an exercise for the Germans. Whereas the past two Youth World Cup finals had ended in dog fights right through to the end, this one was to be totally one-sided. Money was no longer a factor. The skill and tactical play exhibited by the West Germans sent the Arabs home with only a dream. It was a clinic of sorts, as the West German team, efficient as a Mercedes Benz, went up and down the wet field with precise passing and movement, winning 4–0. By no means was this an embarrassment to Qatar, though. What they had accomplished will be recorded in the

Top: The youth team in Bellinzona, Switzerland, in 1979; Bottom: At the U.S. Olympic Training Center before the U.S.-Canada game, won by the U.S. 3–0.

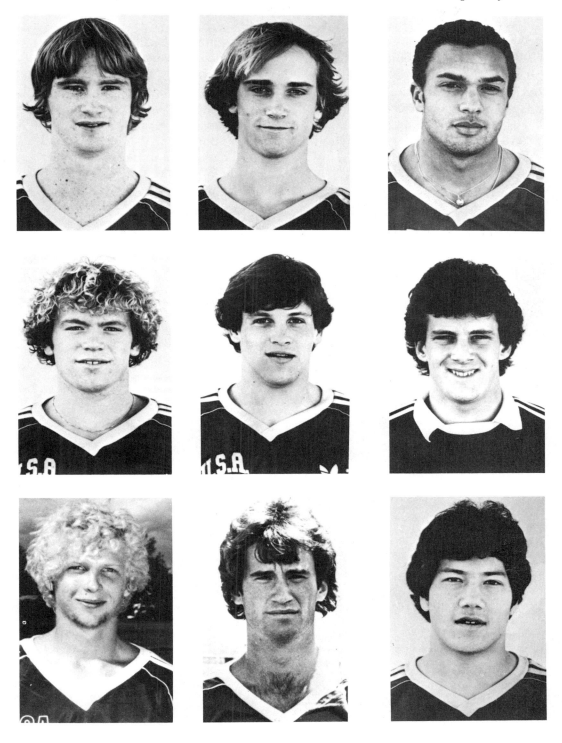

Top row: Jay Ainslie, Tom Kain, Darryl Gee; Second row: Tom Gardiner, John Stollmeyer, Craig Scarpelli; Bottom row: Mark Devey, Bill McKeon, David Lischner.

books forever. No person with any knowledge of soccer would ever have suggested that Qatar would have made it to the final. Remember, Qatar only managed a tie against the U.S., and that was the result of a highly disputed goal.

Prior to leaving for Australia from Duisberg, Germany, with the U.S. team, Bob Gansler and I observed the West German coaching staff preparing their youth team for the 1983 World Youth Championship. Most of the players were born in 1962, 1963, and 1964. They had come from eight different regions for an interregional tournament, in order to be screened by the coaching staff. As the U.S. squad left for Australia, no one back in the States was organizing the next national youth team.

V

What You Should Know About U.S. Soccer

THE GROWTH AND DEVELOPMENT OF THE AMERICAN SOCCER PLAYER IS A MAJOR priority of the USSF and its membership. As a governing body for soccer in America, its efforts are placed directly into the structuring and formation of youth teams, senior leagues, and player-development programs. Consequently, the raising of American players, directly or indirectly, is on their shoulders.

Very little was accomplished in the growth and development of American players until the early seventies. But since this time, the progress and growth of the players accelerated tremendously relative to what was there in the beginning.

The first goal scored by an American on a full-side American team in Western Europe was scored by Perry Van Der Beck against West Germany in the Prince Rainier Tournament in Monaco in the fall of 1977. Since the 1950 World Cup victory of the U.S. over England in Brazil, several other positive things had happened in U.S. national team programs—the qualification of the U.S. team for the 1972 Olympics in Munich, and, in 1973, the 1–0 U.S. victory over Poland in Hartford. In 1980, for the first time, the U.S. team won a full-side international in Eastern Europe—beating Hungary 2–0.

To use an objective barometer of the nation's soccer progress, I was a member of the U.S. team when England dealt the U.S. a 10–0 defeat at Randall's Island, N.Y. In 1980, the U.S. team played at Manchester against England "B" and, even with a poor performance, lost only 1–0. To make the picture clearer, our youth team lost 8–1 to Mexico in Puerto Rico in the 1976 Youth World Cup qualifying matches. The 1980 result of the U.S. team that did qualify was dramatically different.

In fact, in recent years, the U.S. teams (World Cup, Olympic, and Youth) have been on a parity with their competitors in the CONCACAF region. (We must remember that in the mid-70s the U.S. teams had difficulty winning over small countries such as Bermuda.)

So, now that this has been accomplished, there is a need to look into future planning and the development of American players. If we continue to work at the pace we have set over the past few years, then our growth will only be the same. We will continue to be competitive in the CONCACAF region. However, we will not come close to the final step, and that is Argentina, Germany, England, Holland, etc. Obviously then, changes need to be made and improvement accelerated.

On the youth level, where there

seems to be a reasonable, organized method administratively, there is a need to better the program for our players. Creating state and regional team tournaments and opening national training centers for the elite players should be the top priorities, and the elite players should be given an increasing number of opportunities to compete internationally.

The Olympic team development should be of major concern to all. The 1984 Olympics will be hosted by the U.S., which means that the U.S. soccer team is an automatic qualifier. It is quite possible that the Olympic team could be made up of players under twenty years of age. A U.S. v. Soviet game at the Los Angeles Coliseum in 1984 could be a total disaster for U.S. soccer. The question is, What do we do? First and foremost, recognize the problem and, for the coming years, be prepared to challenge it.

The national team, having reached equality in the CONCACAF region, now needs to challenge the best. This can no longer be accomplished by the old method, the one that has taken us this far. A different approach is now required, since the old method cannot be improved upon.

The solution could be in selecting the elite American players, placing them in one concentrated program over the next four years, training these players as a controlled group—adding and subtracting whenever required, and then, finally, challenging the best. Having a controlled group of thirty to forty players over eleven months a year playing, for example, thirty games in the NASL plus ten international games

in the fall and winter, is a realistic solution to the problem. Only under circumstances such as these can we challenge the rest of the world and have our dreams come true.

Player Analysis

The 1980 American soccer player can easily be evaluated, and a prognosis of his abilities can be determined, through a simple methodical approach that ends to an accurate assessment. Four components of soccer coaching are used in observing the American soccer player: *fitness, technique, tactics,* and *psychology.*

The Physical. The American athlete, from a physical point of view, is better developed than any other athlete in the world. However, the American soccer player is poorest developed in the sense of a soccer physical development. The obvious reason is that his exposure to the game and the ball is insufficient.

Any soccer player that has dreams and expectations of playing international or professional soccer needs, on a daily basis from age five, to attend to body movement related to the ball. Anything less than that minimizes his growth in physical soccer player develoment. This type of environment, unfortunately, is not evident in America today. Our players are still very much part-timers in the true sense of the word.

The blame for this lack of soccer development is not all the fault of the players or the USSF. The general physical education curriculum nationally does not lend itself to pure soccer physical development. In this development, we simply are looking for agility, flexibility, ball feel or touch, and, mainly, educating muscles for soccer through daily exposure.

Comparative studies have been administered between a control group of elementary school children in Europe playing soccer, European handball, and gymnastics, and an equivalent control group of American children playing softball, touch football, and basketball. The soccer physical development was significantly 60 percent higher in the European children. This study alone indicates where one of the major problems exists in the U.S. soccer player's development.

Understanding soccer physical development lends to rapid growth and learning of other components. The purist often will say, "We learned on our own, without any coaching." The answer to that statement is with a question. "How much better could you have been, if, in fact, you had the proper training environment for soccer players?" The gut feeling of soccer people is not nonexistent in such soccer powers as Germany, Italy, Holland, etc. There is a science to this game of soccer, and it needs to be studied, understood, and implemented.

The Technical. The frequently used statement in our coaching schools is that the American soccer player plays too slowly. This simply means that because of the inherent problem in his physical development, his technical speed is too slow for national and international competition. To improve in technical speed, again, requires day-to-day training in a controlled situation supervised by a soccer coach.

Our inability to create a sufficient supply of information (pictures, movies, players, coaches) about technical training for the 2 million or so soccer youngsters only places our development deeper behind the eight ball. Acquiring incorrect technique in soccer lends to a poorly skilled player who plays too slowly for higher standards of competition.

The Tactical. The American player, for the most part, is intelligent because of his learning experience in school or college. However, it is important to recognize that there exists a type of intelligence for different areas of concentration. There is a soccer intelligence. General intelligence to understand and comprehend the situation at hand is necessarily coupled with soccer intelligence to create or solve a problem.

Our players lack the latter. Their ability to solve or create tactical problems is also too slow. This again is related to the problems at hand with physical upbringing and slow technical play. The environment that is needed to improve the mental concentration and quick thinking process of American players is day-to-day training with competition. Anything less than that makes them slow thinkers.

The Psychological. The American player is a very naive, raw soccer person in the world of soccer. The principles on which he is raised in the American social structure of fair play and honest competition fall short when he is exposed to international play. This creates a problem for him, and he is tormented with feelings of fair play and retaliation when the adversary plays the role of a *macho*. The younger American players are totally confused, and, normally, it requires two to three years before they begin to understand international soccer.

The lack of competition and playing time on a year-round basis by American players results in a loss of their competitive spirit and drive. Intensity can be sustained only through competition and exposure to pressure. The older our player becomes, the less intense he is in his game. This was evident in our last World Cup matches where the likes of Ricky Davis and Larry Hulcer demonstrated very little competitive spirit as opposed to three or four years ago when they played for the Olympic "B" team.

The development of soccer players in America over the past few years demonstrates that we, despite many outside obstacles, were able to develop a small number of quality players. These players more readily developed in the defense and midfield. Some players were converted in the course of their growth from position to position. The most difficult area of development is in the attack and, specifically, finishing. This area requires the highest concentration of training and it is the most difficult area to play in because of the time and space allowed.

The best technical players in the world are not the Beckenbauers, but, in fact, are players such as Gerd Müller, Trevor Francis, and Karl Heinz Rummenigge. These players demonstrate the highest technical execution in areas where it is most difficult to play. The world is sometimes fooled by players who play so attractively in open space!

In America, we are not even close to developing such players who can finish and bring results. We should not raise our expectations immediately. The Australian experience showed our players what the world-class players and teams are made of. This type of learning produces world-class players. We need to reach the finals more often.

There is a science in the development of a soccer player. Germany has demonsrated this method to its fullest. On the other hand, we can argue and questions whether this science has ever been applied in Brazil, Argentina, etc. The answer is no. Their players, on the whole, are developed from the gut-level approach—throw the ball out and let them play. This method can also work, but only if the conditions for it are provided. By that I mean, if you have all your top athletes from age six kicking and playing three v. three in their backyards, there is no doubt that some will evolve as world class players. However, the ultimate qustions is asked, How many will miss making the grade? Fortunately or unfortunately, we do not provide an atmosphere for this type of development and, therefore, must approach it another way. And this situation probably will not change during our lifetimes.

Coaching Philosophy

One of the most important consider-ations in attempting to develop a national coaching scheme is to formulate and disseminate a philosophy that is conducive for all american players and coaches. This philosophy is strictly designed for the American soccer community and should not be compared to other soccer countries and their beliefs. We are different, and our problems and our circumstances are unique. Therefore, our thinking must be geared differently.

It is almost a world-accepted fact that modern soccer should be played totally, which means ten players in the attack and ten players in the defense. This style of "total soccer" possibly became recognized in the middle seventies when Holland, with Cruyff and company, was running over all countries by utilizing defenders in the attack and vice versa. Consequently, because of the media and their observations, everyone became involved in talking about total soccer.

The fact is that there is no total soccer, nor does any country demonstrate this style. Holland and Germany come close—the other countries play, for the most part, programmed and positional. To play total soccer, you must have total soccer players. There are very few players in the world of this calibre.

This leads me to explain the philosphy for American soccer development. The intent and purpose is to develop each player to his fullest potential—bringing out of him all the fine qualities he possesses as a soccer player. Therefore, the quest is to develop this player totally. Once we have accomplished the player's total development—physically, technically, tactically, and psychologically—we can then begin to develop a style that is suited for him, possibly total soccer.

This type of development is what the American soccer community must concentrate on, creating total soccer players. The game of soccer in America can then begin to acquire a style for American players that would be attractive, efficient, and purposeful. Once that has become a reality, we can begin to challenge the rest of the world.

The intent is to bring the most out of each individual and provide an opportunity for him to demonstrate his talent. Size is not a factor; Ricky Davis has demonstrated that, at 5'8", he can potentially be a big player. The best player in the world currently is Karl Heinz Rummenigge, who is 6'1".

A Coaching Continuity

Impatience on the part of the entire U.S. soccer community has become a very significant characteristic. The constant question, "When will the U.S. become an international power?", is on the tip of everyone's tongue who deals with soccer.

Those directly involved with U.S. problems and some of the experts from abroad have given us a projected number of years before we will reach success. A consensus shows that ten years is the magic number. This ten-year prediction started sometime in 1966 and, of course, we still hear the ten-year figure today.

To overcome some of these obstacles we need to develop a coaching continuity in international play. We all expect instant success because the number of participants has skyrocketed. The numbers alone are not the answer. Part of the answer is having our coaches follow a suitable method that is applicable to our international player development.

We are, realistically, a very young country in soccer and have not developed a coaching continuity. Too few of our coaches have been exposed to international play as players, and consequently our coaches are not fully aware of what is happening on that level. This, of course, is not the fault of our coaches but definitely our system. If our aim is to develop players of international calibre, then the easiest way would be to have the players play in international competition and also to have these players exposed, prior to their international competition to American coaches who played previously on our World Cup, Olympic, Pan American, and National Youth Teams.

If we were to study the success of West Germany, and we should study their success since at the moment they are number one in the world and play very attractive soccer, we would find a coaching continuity or pattern that began in the early 1950s under Sepp Herberger. This sytem has finally arrived in full swing in Germany. He alone did not make things happen, but people under him who were players and later became coaches, made West Germany such a success. The players of the 1950s who played internationally became coaches of the 1960s, and the players of the 1960s became coaches of the 1970s. All along there was a professional follow-up of international players becoming coaches.

The development of a soccer player is faster and more complete when he is fortunate to have a coach who not only is a professional teacher and coach but also one with international game experience. Our system provides very little of this—for many reasons. Our international games in the past were

very few and far between. The World Cup and the Olympics are staged every four years. We are not involved in any international cup competition such as the European and South American Cups. Consequently, we only have a limited number of players who played under those conditions. West Germany, being involved in a number of club cups—continent cups plus the World Cup—can provide a large number of players with that sort of exposure, and these players eventually become coaches.

If we were to look at our National Team players of the past, we would find very few who are currently coaching—Harry Keough, Bob Kehoe, Matt Bahr, Jim Benedek, Al Trost, Pat McBride, and a few others, but that is all. So, in twenty-seven years, we have only those few with international playing and coaching experience. Needless to say, this is another consideration that has slowed our growth in international play. This, I'm sure, will change rapidly, and already we see some improvement. The past few years the national coaching school staff has witnessed some twenty to thirty former and present national team players in the coaching course. This is a positive sign. These coaches will add a whole new dimension to our development of players of international calibre.

On our current Youth Team we have two players who will receive our "C" license once they are of age. We have four or five Olympic Team players in the same category. In the future, we hope to see more of this type of development. If we can combine the quality coaching of our domestic coaches with the refinement of our players by former international players and now coaches, we can safely knock off a few more years from the magic ten-year evolution.

More about American Players

Different tests have been administered to the National Team players in recent years.

Pure Speed Test

This test was administered to different players of the Youth, Olympic, and Senior squads. The test is a fifty-yard sprint from a moving start. On the Olympic and National teams, all players fell into the average of 4.8 to 5.2 seconds. This speed was comparable to different European team players. Doc Lawson (Philadelphia Fever) had the best time of all U.S. players. He was clocked at 4.5 seconds.

Acceleration Test

This is a four-second sprint test to measure how many yards a player can gain. The player stands on the starting line with his back to the line. He then sprints as far as he can go in the four seconds. The American players average between twenty-eight and thirty-one yards.

Vertical Jump Test (Sergeant Jump Test)

In the vertical jump test, the U.S. players were above the average of the European players. The Americans averaged twenty-four to twenty-six inches, as compared with the Europeans'

average of twenty-three to twenty-five inches. The highest vertical jump was recorded by Doc Lawson and Mark McKain.

The Cooper Test

This test determines general endurance, measuring the distance gained when running for twelve minutes. The American players averaged between 1.9 miles and 2.2 miles. These results were on par with the performance of Brazilian National team players. East Germany's National Team players had higher scores in the Cooper test.

Shooting for Power Test

This test was administered in Paris two days prior to the U.S.-France game, to measure the most powerful shooters on both teams. The ball was kicked from a dead position eighteen yards from the goal net, which was attached firmly to the goal posts as in an inverted trampoline effect. A French-designed Tachyfoot machine was used to determine the results. Doc Lawson scored the highest with a 78 m.p.h. kick. Lacombe of France was second.

Nutrition

Tests administered to a U.S. under-21 team in 1977 at the Lake Tahoe Olympic Training Center indicated that soccer players burned up 5,000 to 6,500 calories per day. The training was twice per day, one and one-half hours in duration. In the morning, training was of a technical nature and in the evening, it was of a tactical nature. The technical training included incorporation of fitness as well.

Skill Training of American Players

This type of training can best be achieved under conditions where there is no fatigue. Execution of game skills can be best accomplished under the pressure of an opponent, i.e., match-related. The most important consideration in improving the technical part of the American player's game is to improve his foot speed. Once this condition is improved, his passing, shooting, and dribbling will improve to international standards. Approximately half of the skills involved in the game of soccer require kicking and one-third require receiving and possession.

Mental Process of Players

Every player is involved in two decision-making theories—individual decision-making theory and game theory. With the American player, we need to know and understand whether the player has enough information to warrant deciding on a particular move and whether he knows of the possible alternatives available to him. The presence, or absence, of one or both determines the amount of risk involved in the final execution. The experienced players have the edge in this category. The American players need more playing time. Three to six months is only one-fourth to one-half of the time put in by European players. Mental speed is as important as pure speed and foot speed. The American player is in dire need of improvement in all three areas.

Ball Contacts

The highest number of ball contacts by an individual player in international competition was achieved by Perry Van Der Beck in a Youth World Cup qualifying match in Hondurdas against Trinidad. Perry had twenty-two contacts in the first half and twenty-five contacts in the second half. This was exceptionally high for an American. On the average, a European player makes contact with the ball every two and one-half minutes.

Physical Size

One of the most difficult problems that some of the American players experience in their technical training stems from the fact that their lower extremities are not proportionately equal. This simply means that the player's femur bone is longer than his tibia or vice versa. If this is a factor, then the mechanical movement of the knee joint could affect the player's ability to execute kicking for distance or accuracy. It is important to recognize this physical problem and make adjustments in the player's technical training.

The Indoor Game

The indoor game has been around for decades in the U.S. and throughout the world. It has been played in different gymnasiums, armories, and arenas. It had significant popularity on the East Coast, as well as in the St. Louis and Chicago areas. In St. Louis, the game was called hoc-soc. The East Coast, particularly the New York metropolitan area and Philadelphia, had organized leagues during the winter break. The American League and the German American League staged regular indoor tournaments on Wednesdays and Fridays in the New York Armory, Patterson Armory, and the Jersey City Armory. The tournaments were eight to ten weeks in duration. The rules were the same as the outdoor game. There were no dasher boards to play the ball off, and when the ball went out of bounds it resulted in a kick-in.

One major indoor soccer tournament was held in 1958 by the American Soccer League at Madison Square Garden. The league was permitted to stage an all-day tournament on hard soil following a Roy Rogers horse show. The dasher boards were used, however, the goals were not imbedded into the wall. Any ball going behind the goal was not in play. The all-day tournament attracted over 14,000 people. The winner was the Uhrik Truckers Soccer Club from Philadelphia. They defeated the Philadelphia Ukrainian Nationals by a score of 11–9.

The Europeans and Latin Americans have also indulged in indoor soccer, although not on a very serious level. They merely used the indoor game as a means of keeping players fit for the outdoor season. Brazil, though, does have an organized indoor league and, as a result, has developed indoor soccer players who to a great degree can only play the indoor game.

In 1974, the Philadelphia Atoms (NASL) experimented with indoor soccer, playing against the Red Army team from the Soviet Union. It was a big success; 16,000 spectators witnessed a very exciting game. The game was played at the Philadelphia Spectrum on the AstroTurf-covered ice rink. The goal was a cage with dimensions of 4 feet by 16 feet—somewhat of a handicap to the goalies, who had to take on the posture of a hunchback. Nevertheless, it was exciting. The NASL subsequently staged several winter tournaments in 1975 and 1976.

The first offical indoor soccer league in the world was formed in 1978 in the U.S. The Major Indoor Soccer League, under the leadership of Earl Foreman (commissioner) and Ed Tepper (owner of the New Jersey Rockets) formed a six-team professional league with Philadelphia, New York, Houston, Cleveland, Cincinnati, and Pittsburgh as charter members. I was hired as a consultant to the league and prepared the rules as well as reconstructed the goal, with new dimensions of $6\frac{1}{2}$ feet by 12 feet. This present indoor goal allows the goalie to perform in an upright position and allows for goals scored off headers. In 1979, Dr. Joe Machnik was hired as a full-time chief referee and director of operations for the MISL. The league now has thirteen members and is looking to increase its membership to sixteen by 1983.

The St. Louis Steamers have created a miracle on the indoor soccer turf, averaging well over 18,000 spectators at home during the 1981 season. The team is mostly made up of American players from the U.S. National Team, and they are one of the top teams in the league. The New York Arrows, with their superstar Steve Zungul, have won three consecutive championships in the MISL. Zungul has set scoring records that will be in the MISL books for a long time to come. Several other superstars have emerged—at Pittsburgh, Stan Terlecki is on the heels of Zungul for the scoring title. Shep Messing, from the U.S. Olympic Team and the New York Cosmos, is now the premier goalie in the league.

Several other Americans have taken positions with their teams: Joe Fink at Baltimore, Dave MacWilliams at the Philadelphia Fever, O'Hara at Pittsburgh, and Steve Pecher and Tony Bellinger at St. Louis.

FIFA is keeping a close watch on the American indoor soccer scene. The attendance in the league's fourth year is still climbing. The league average during the 1981-82 season nears 9,000 per game. The future is bright, and FIFA, I'm sure, would like to be a part of that future. There is strong evidence that within the next couple of years FIFA will stage an "Indoor World Cup." With the U.S. having some of the finest indoor facilities in the world, it would be no surprise if such a competition were staged here. A tournament of this type would insure the continued success of the MISL and would spur the growth of the game not only nationally but internationally as well.

One can easily foresee international matches played between American club teams as well as National Teams in the very near future. Exciting times are ahead for indoor soccer. The soccer purists have difficulty accepting the sport, for they have never played it. However, a new generation of American fans is growing rapidly, and their commitment and enthusiasm for the game will insure its existence for a long time to come.

VI
Styles and Trends in World Cup Soccer: The Technical and the Tactical

I T SEEMS AS THOUGH ALMOST ANYONE WILL TELL YOU THAT SOCCER IS A GAME OF both attack and defense. To be obsessed with this statement is fundamentally incorrect.

There was a time in soccer's history when goals came in large numbers. As the game became more sophisticated, the offensive raids on goal were curtailed. We will touch on many reasons why the attack was surpressed, but for the moment we need to expand on the opening statement.

Because players are taught to exhibit a dual role—both in the attack and on defense—the chances of greater goal-scoring opportunities are already minimized. In the early years of soccer growth and development, tactics were hardly considered. Overall strategy and skill were the prevailing factors in determining a team's success. As the game grew, and professional soccer was just around the corner, coaches and managers began to innovate new means of surviving. Initially, it was offensive exploitation. This was due to the laws of the game, in particular, the offside rule. However, changes were made to lower scoring opportunities, resulting in a new offside law. This marked the beginning of introducing player formations, which would either improve scoring or deny it. The game of soccer became a huge chess game of playing safe or playing to score. On paper, all chess moves work, but nothing works quite the same when the opponent is introduced into the picture. Slowly, famous coaches became known to the world because of their game tactics. Moving players into certain positions to open attacks or close down attacks was the beginning of the development of systems of play. A system is an organization of eleven players on a soccer field. In modern soccer, a team will align itself with a goalie and usually four defenders, at least two in the middle, and two up front. The other two players are positioned in accordance with the team's physical and technical capabilities—and that of the opponent.

Coaches such as Carl Rappan (Swiss Bolt), Chapman of England (W. M. formation), and Herrera with the catenaccio (see drawing at the end of this chapter) are all world-renowned for their formations. Most of these formations were designed to prevent goals for one main reason—job security. A 1-0 win is better than a loss and a 1-1 tie away from home is also better than a loss. The coaches and managers were looking for security, and you can't blame them.

Now we need to delve further into the soccer player's development to see why the game is struggling in so many areas of the world, both financially and in an artistic and finishing sense. It became very apparent in the early sixties that the emphasis would be on defensive play. Whether this would be accomplished with numerical superiority or through careful selection of players is irrelevant. The main purpose as to play destructive soccer, i.e., not allowing goal-scoring opportunities. The main reason for this type of play was, and is, that the clubs are playing for high stakes.

FIFA and soccer in general has prided itself on the fact that the seventeen laws of the game have been around for decades with only minor adjustments. One wonders and questions whether or not this lack of change has really been an obstacle to the improvement of the game. Observing other sports in America, one finds that changes or adjustments are made almost on a yearly basis.
These are made only in an effort to benefit the sport—both for the players and the spectators. Not to belabor the point, but we only have to look at the reality of soccer and its problems. As coaches continue to play defensively, defending with eight and attacking with two, the results will continue to be consistently low, 1-0, 1-1, 0-0, etc.

Therefore, a serious study must be made investigating ways of circumventing this problem created by coaches. Nowhere in the world will you find a coach that is willing to attack with numbers if the opponent is in the bunker. A study on rule changes to modify game strategies to include a greater number of attacks can be the only answer. Looking into areas such as the size of the field, size of the goal, offside rules, violent fouls, limiting the number of defenders in specified areas must take place. A survey of national coaches competing in the 1966 World Cup predicted that the games would be defensive. They were, with the teams consistently defending with superior numbers, aggressively tackling. The modern defender is so skillful that he is willing to hold the ball in his defensive third with confidence. This is because he knows his skill is on par with the opponent's attackers. In addition, the defender is as quick, strong, and agile as the attacker. Only rule changes in the game can alleviate some of the problems of the modern game.

In recent studies of competition of teams in the World Cup (1962 through 1978), observations were made regarding the success of penetrating attacks. Again, because of the principles of play followed by individual players (whereby a player or team, having lost possession of the ball, does an immediate chase to regain or get goalside), the team falls into a defensive screen.

If both teams are attacking with three and defending with seven, this only creates much square and back passing between defenders and midfielders before an attack is staged. It is also apparent that many teams will try to lure the attacking team into its webb, and then, while gaining possession of the ball, they will counterattack. This attacking system is useful, for it allows for teams to counterattack with three to three and one-half players against the opponent's three defenders in an area 60 by 75 yards. This means that there is much space, creating the best possibilities for scoring. However, those that understand this strategy will not be deceived and will attack with fewer numbers and, of course, with caution. There have been games played in the seventies where a great number of penetrating attacks were executed. If a team decides to go directly to goal over midfield play, this frequently causes penetrating opportunities, particularly if a team has a "tall target" player to whom the ball can be played from a distance. Other ways of creating penetrating attacks are through soccer personalities. One of these personalities was Johan Cruyff, who was capable of creating attacks almost at will. The soccer world will have a long wait before another player of such great talent comes along.

By observing the performance of the two top teams in the 1974 World Cup, West Germany and the Netherlands, one finds that even teams with capabilities of making penetrating attacks still finish with low scoring games. West Germany playing against Chile in 1974 had fifty-one penetrating attacks over Chile's sixteen, and had twenty attempts to score over Chile's seven. The only goal that was actually scored was by Breitner on a thirty-yard rocket into the upper corner of the net. West Germany played against East Germany and had fifty-three penetrating attacks as compared with East Germany's twenty attacks. West Germany lost 1–0 on a counterattack goal from the goalkeeper to the winger, who went in and scored. The Netherlands in some of their games

showed even a greater number of attacks against their opponents, but still the results were generally low-scoring games. Against Sweden, Holland staged sixty-one raids on the Swedes' goal as compared with ten attacks by Sweden. The final score was 0–0, with Sweden missing two breakaways in the first half of the game. The Swedes for a long time defended with nine players, and the Dutch had difficulty scoring. Using these two teams as examples and studying their performance, it is obvious that even though a team is superior in quality, the opponent—less skillful as they may be—still has an excellent opportunity to survive. For the past thirty years or so, most goals have been scored from restart situations—corner kicks and free kicks create between sixty-five and seventy percent of the goals in most competitions. The reason for such a high percentage is that teams or players can execute with more precision because the ball is not moving; it is a dead-ball situation. From a dead ball, a player can make better timed runs, set up screens, and utilize his shooting skills with better concentration and accuracy. It was apparent in the 1974 World Cup, and for that matter, in most of the cups over the past twenty years, that teams having speedy front runners playing wide where there is more space, can bring balls to the touchline and serve them into the penalty area to other onrushing front runners for scores. Poland was a good example of such attacks in 1974, as they utilized their wingers—Lato and Gadocha— to the fullest and were able to finish third best in the world.

Incorporation of more players in exchanging positions while the ball is moving was a new and exciting way of playing exhibited by some nations, in particular, Holland. Cruyff was the center of attraction in the whirlpool system of play. Balls were played up to him from the back and then players raced into new spaces without hesitation. They ran with confidence because percentages indicated that Cruyff would not lose possession of the ball. This type of play brought raves from around the world. However, very few countries could copy this style. There was only one Cruyff in the seventies, and he could only play for one team.

The South American teams have a habit of spending long periods of time at midfield, with close interpassing to feet, often with one-touch, flicking the ball to a teammate before looking for a penetrating pass. It appears on occasion that one could remove the goalposts and the players involved with the ball at midfeld would not miss it. The notion behind the long interpassing on one side of the half is to free or open the other side for runs from behind. Close interpassing is prey, however, for strong aggressive European tackling. Brazil demonstrated a high standard of ball movement at the back and midfield in 1974. However, their penetration was almost nonexistent. They hardly scored except from restarts. In this type of interpassing for a long period of time, the opponent begins to read and understand the deft one-touch flicks, and begins to tackle more quickly and assuredly. By doing so, the rhythm of a team or a player is destroyed. Consequently, the buildup does not materialize. Latin American players play brilliantly when everything is going

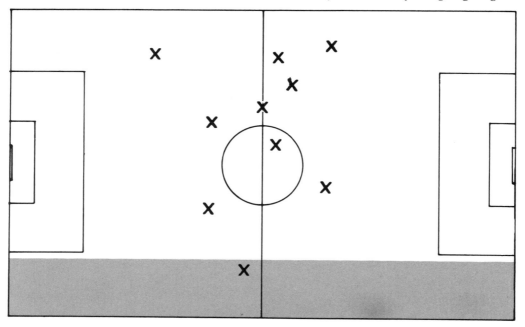

In the South American style of play, players are concentrated on one side of the field where the ball is interpassed among five or six players, leaving the other side open, thus creating space to run from behind.

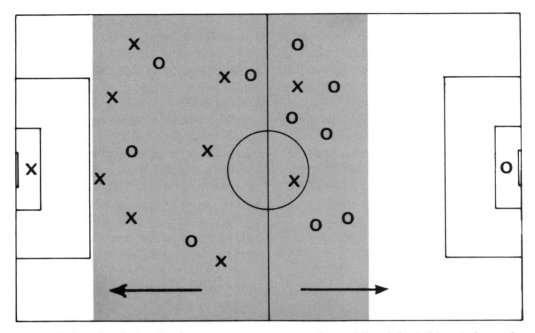

In the English style of play, both teams are compact in the middle of the field and always have five to six players between the ball and their goal.

well. However, when they are denied their game, they tend to become individualistic and frustrated.

European players seldom attain the high level of personal performance achieved by the Latins. However, as teams, they often rise to the occasion when they are in a losing posture and try to overthrow the opponent with sheer energy. In Europe, there is a mixture of styles and tactics.

Sweden and East Germany rely on classic defensive adjustments with long passes to forwards who can break through on their own. The purpose of this style is to isolate one-on-one or three-on-three situations at halffield, thus leaving the forwards to operate in an area where there are only six or seven players involved in total. It is simpler to play under those circumstances—where there are fewer players, there are fewer problems to resolve.

The English style is based on hard power tackling and an abundance of players in the middle of the field. The expression "push out" on a clearance is a typical English play. You will find six or more defenders getting themselves between the ball and the goal when the other team is in possession. Attacking raids are often made on the flanks by fast forwards or players coming from behind. The serve is often high across the face of the goal. Most teams have big robust center forwards, or target men, who can jump high to head the ball and shoot from all angles and distances.

West Germany has difficulty handling the English style of play. In

European club competitions for cup tournaments, the English teams are often more successful against the West Germans because of the high pressure game the Brits employ. However, in general, the West German game appears to be the most attractive and efficient of them all. They play fast with one-touch interpassing at midfield, with quick buildups on the attack to create space for players to receive productive passes. The one-two passes are their style of attack. Their man-to-man marking makes the game more alive and dynamic. It is the boring, yawn-yawn, type of games played in many parts of the world, where teams fall back into deep zones to protect their goals, that are partially responsible for the drop in attendances.

In Italy, every team is prepared in defensive tactics to retreat on goal, and,

in the defensive third, to mark man-to-man. One of the countries most successful in breaking the Italian defensive system was Poland in 1974. Poland had world-class wingers who could bring the ball from the flanks into the opponent's penalty area to create scoring opportunities. While there is space available on the flanks when the "catenaccio" is employed by a team, there are not that many great wingers who are capable of "going around the corner" of a defense to serve the ball into the danger zone. Generally speaking, when the "catenaccio" system is used, low scores result.

With the exception of Yugoslavia, and at times Czechoslovakia, the Eastern European countries, such as the Soviet Union, Romania, Bulgaria, Albania, etc., play a very methodical, programmed style. Their movements

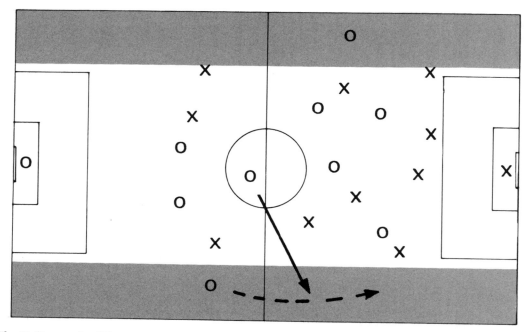

The Italian style, "Catenaccio," is compact in the back with seven players marking tight. The flanks are open.

are very predictable, and there is very little individuality in their style of play. This, of course, stems from the social structure of the countries themselves. The teams that are successful in those countries have a player or players with flair, who can improvise and score. Oleg Blohin, a front runner for Dynamo Kiev in the Ukraine, is the most colorful player in all of Eastern Europe. Because of his abilities, his team wins the championship in the Soviet Union's professional—or should we say amateur—league year in and year out. (A close friend from Eastern Europe once explained to me with a bit of sarcasm, that they don't have professionalism in their country—that's why their players want to form a players' union.)

The most contrasting style to that of Eastern Europe is played by the Dutch. Their ability to send penetrating passes into space to onrushing players at full speed made Holland a very famous soccer country during the seventies. The Dutch players' confidence and sports arrogance made them a most dangerous side. In particular, their forwards demonstrated a superior ability to regain the ball once it was lost to an opponent. Normally, forwards are content to position themselves in the defensive role in front of the opponent with the ball, thereby blocking his path and forcing him to pass. The Dutch forwards, however, immediately went into tackles, sometimes winning possession of the ball. Even if they didn't gain possession, they would force the opponent to pass the ball quickly. Consequently, the precision of the pass was often faulty, resulting in an interception. This kind of play,

involving all players on the team is called "total soccer."

As it was mentioned earlier, systems and styles of play usually revolve around world-class soccer players. Reflecting back, we can ascertain that Puskas and Company created a style that was admired and copied by all of Europe. In England, Matthews made the wing play a part of the strategy employed by all British clubs., His ability to lose defenders with finesse and ease was respected by all. Later, it was DiStefano who introduced a wrinkle into the game, by going deep into his defensive third to collect balls. Pele made the Brazilian 4–2–4 formation a way of life in Latin American soccer, and it is used still to this day. Franz Beckenbauer made the role of sweeper world famous. The Dutch became a dynamic soccer power because of Cruyff, who was probably the closest to being a complete player. His physical qualities of pure speed, acceleration, and agility surpassed that of any player. Technically very sound, with excellent ball control and accurate passing under pressure, his superior ability has yet to be duplicated. Tactically, he was a soccer genius with leadership qualities, that required little if any coaching. On the field, he was the coach.

Future Trends

A great concern is expressed by professional clubs, managers, and coaches regarding the declining attendance around the world. As we discussed, one of the reasons for this is most likely the defensive tactics employed by teams. In particular, in the U.S., where soccer fields tend to be narrower, defensive strategies are built into the game. The converted football and baseball stadia are, on the average, 60 by 110 yards, as compared with the ideal of 75 by 120 yards. This automatically reduces the space available for offensive tactics, turning the game into a defensive war. Franz Beckenbauer was never especially pleased about traveling to Memphis (58 by 110 yards), where his potential was drastically diminished because his style of play was better suited to a larger field.

Television and the world economy have contributed to the dwindling attendance. Other recreational activities in certain countries have taken the spectator out of the stadium. Fortunately, there is plenty of evidence that soccer is continuing to grow in participation, particularly in the United States. Youth registrations in the United States Soccer Federation were up almost 20 percent in 1981 over the previous year. Women have taken a much more active role in the game, and women's leagues are on the rise at the high-school and collegiate levels. This new trend will play an important role in maintaining the popularity of the sport.

Unfortunately, because of the large number of recreational activities available in the more affluent countries, the young player does not dedicate enough time to improving his skills on a year-round basis. There is a need to provide more and better playing fields for our youth and adults, both for recreational and competitive purposes.

Small-sided games on smaller fields are an important consideration for the future. Playing six-a-side soccer gives young players more touches of the ball, allowing for more rapid skill development. Indoor soccer, in areas where climate is a factor, will be important to the development of the sport, especially in underdeveloped soccer countries such as the U.S. and Canada. Recreational soccer will be the event of the future for both physical conditioning and mental regeneration. Let us hope that from this "social soccer," new soccer spectators and enthusiasts will come forth.

The World Cup plays an important role in providing added life to soccer in underdeveloped countries. National and international news media spread the word of the World Cup competition in Spain, and young athletes from lower middle classes begin to identify with the game. The American black athlete will contribute to the success of American soccer both on the national and international levels of play. Talents like Al Smith and Darryl Gee, both members of the U.S. National Youth Team, will become more prominent.

There are signs that the South Americans are trying to develop the European style of teamwork with determined competitive spirit. On the other hand, the Europeans are attempting to copy the swift and skillful style of the Latins. A blending of the two styles by the United States could eventually make us a world power.

Because of the Dutch commitment to the total-soccer-player concept during the seventies, young players will be better prepared and developed. Perhaps this will eliminate the rigid obsession with 4–2–4, 4–3–3 formations. The American player of the future will more readily identify with the Dutch style of play, making the American game much more exciting.

Countries with higher academic and economic standards will have an influence on the soccer player's development. More intelligent soccer players will bring the game up still another level. Sports medicine will provide all the physical means to improve the players' physical capabilities.

In forming a team, it is sound to have strength "up the middle." An excellent goalkeeper, an active sweeper, two skillful midfielders and at least one powerful scorer would be the ideal. In the future, there will be enough quality players to show strength all over the field.

The future players will be able to play faster in tight spaces, will be more expressive in technique, and will be able to execute skills under full speed. Germany and Holland are good examples of countries that have developed large numbers of quality players because of their modern training methods. Coaching schools around the world will be encouraged to develop quality coaches who, in turn, will be responsible for developing total players. The one-way players are slowly disappearing. Players, as we have seen, must be able to attack and defend at will, using the entire field of play. The timing of runs and reading of the game will be on a higher level than ever before because of better mental training. At the same time, you will see drastic improvements in concentration and anticipation.

In the 1974 and 1978 World Cups, more balls were turned over through interceptions than by tackling. This is surely evidence of the trend toward better concentration and anticipation on the part of national team players. Tight marking has become the defensive style of the decade, and this will continue to be true. However, as players are exposed to more and more of this, so too on the attack they will be better prepared to free themselves.

In developing a way of playing in tactical terms, a group of players is certainly more important than the individual. However, within the group, there must be one or more individuals with a high standard of soccer intelligence. This will become more and more evident in the future, and we will see more fluid and efficient tactical patterns.

The world has become a smaller place. Coaches and players will be able to experience more fully the soccer, culture, and tradition of other countries. These experiences will help them to become better coaches and players. Psychology will be utilized more often by our teams and players. The Mexican Youth Team was in training for six months prior to their departure for Australia. In their camp, the team had two full-time psychologists to work with the players. Understanding the soccer player's behavioral patterns and attitudes will help increase his performance. Motivating players will become an easier task than ever before.

Tradition, customs, heredity, etc., have a large effect on National Team play. It is often difficult to change a style of play for these reasons. However, the jet age will create greater opportunities for exposing players to different styles of play, and will make the task that much easier.

Climate plays an important role in a style of play. Countries with warm climatic conditions, such as Brazil and Mexico, tend to play at a slower pace. Adjustment to climate by visiting teams will be made easier through the advanced knowledge brought about by discoveries by sports-medicine specialists. West Germany, for example, did not play to their fullest potential in Gold Cup matches in Uruguay in January 1981 because of the warm temperatures. Their style of play was not suited to the climate.

Contracts and money will have a big influence on soccer. This is particularly true in the U.S., where soccer players will receive, relatively speaking, high salaries for their play. Young players will set goals for themselves to become professionals. The U.S. will play a major part in influencing changes in the laws of the game and could well play a part in bringing spectators back to the game throughout the world. The other dimension in soccer—the indoor game, developed on a professional level in the States—will gain worldwide attention.

VII

A Guide to Mexico City,
Host City of the 1986 World Cup

I F YOU ARE PLANNING ON ATTENDING THE 1986 WORLD CUP FINAL GAMES, THIS information should help you enjoy your trip. First of all, read all the information you receive from the tour you are taking. If you are not going on a tour, and even for those who are, go to your public library and ask the librarian for help in finding out more about Mexico City. There are numerous books and magazine articles about the host city of the World Cup. You would be wise to read several of them to gain a better understanding.

Mexico City is located about 19° north of the Equator and is on a plateau 7,347 feet above sea level. This climate is called a tropical highland, but do not let the name confuse you. You will probably be comfortable in the evenings with a coat or sweater. During the day, a hat will help shield you from the sun's rays. The average temperature in June is 63°. The elevation may cause you some problems during the first day or two of your visit. You can usually overcome this by not overexerting yourself in the beginning. The time in Mexico City is the same as in the Central Time Zone of the States.

Entering Mexico is no problem for the American or Canadian tourist. A birth certificate, notarized affidavit, voter's registration or passport are acceptable proof of identification. If,

however, you are a naturalized citizen, you must carry naturalization papers or a passport. If you have any questions, it is best to check prior to your departure. When you enter Mexico, you will receive a free tourist card.

Upon departing from Mexico, you may be charged a tax of around $3 U.S. at the airport. Check with your travel consultant about this prior to the trip.

Customs regulations are always in flux. Prior to your trip, ask your librarian (or, if you live in a city with a customs office, check as to any changes in the law).

The cuisine of Mexico is outstanding, however, most of the citizens north of the border know "Tex-Mex" rather than true Mexican cooking. For many first timers to Mexico, the change is dramatic and exciting. Traditionally, the Mexicans have five meals a day, but let's stick with the three that we are most familiar with—breakfast, lunch, and dinner. Breakfast is served in most hotels, and the times are set to accommodate you.

The principal meal of the day is served between 2 PM and 4 PM, with a lighter meal served after 8 PM. If you are not accustomed to these hours, most of the hotels and restaurants will be able to accommodate you at an earlier time. However, it is more fun to . . . how do you say it?

. . . "When in Mexico City, do as the Mexicans do."

Some of the best restaurants and shops are located in the Pink Zone (Zona Rosa) of the city. This is a very safe and clean section of the city that caters to Spanish- and non-Spanish-speaking visitors. You may want to consult *Gourmet Cuisine, Bon Appetit,* or some of the guide books for restaurants. You may also check with the hotel manager as to restaurants that they would recommend for dining. You might want to acquaint yourself with these terms to enjoy your food and drink.

FOOD

Carne a la Tampiquena: strips of flank steak grilled over coals, usually served with corn tortillas, fried beans, strips of peppers and onion, and guacamole.

Ceviche: marinated fish appetizer.

Chiles rellenos: large green chile pepper stuffed with minced meat or cheese, dipped in an egg batter and fried; often is served with tomato or green sauce.

Enchilada: tortilla filled with meat or cheese, heated in chile-based sauce.

Frijoles refritos: cooked beans (black, kidney, pinto, pink, etc.), mashed and fried, often with cheese sprinkled on top.

Fruta: fruit; oranges, pineapple, mangos, melons, limes, papayas, and strawberries.

Guacamole: avocado mashed with onions, tomato, chile, and salt; used as a garnish on tacos or with tortillas as an appetizer.

Huachinango a la Veracruzana: red snapper baked in a seasoned sauce of tomatoes, olives, and onions.

Huevos: eggs, often served as *huevos rancheros* (two fried eggs served on a tortilla, spread with fried beans and topped with hot tomato sauce), or *huevos a la Mexicana* (scrambled with green pepper, onions, and tomatoes).

Mole: a rich, dark, aromatic sauce made from ground chocolate with chiles, spices, nuts, and herbs.

Pescado Blanco de Patzcuaro: a fish delicacy; a small white fish from Lake Patzcuaro, sautéed in butter and served with small wedges of lime.

Quesadilla: folded tortilla filled with cheese and lightly fried.

Sopas: soups; soups can be soups or

stews — or as in *sopa seca*, they are a dish of rice or pasta.

Taco: chopped beef, pork, chicken, cheese, etc., folded in to a tortilla, sometimes fried.

Tamale: moist corn masa dough enclosing spicy filling of meat, poultry, etc. and wrapped in corn husks for cooking.

Tortilla: very thin, baked, breadlike patty made from corn masa.

BEVERAGES

Agua: water

Aguas frecas: freshly squeezed fruit drinks.

Brandy: the most popular of Mexican liqueurs.

Cafe: coffee.

Chocolate: chocolate originated in Mexico; one of the best ways to drink it is *chocolate Mexicano*, a combination of chocolate and milk flavored with cinnamon and sugar that is whipped.

Cerveza: beer — some of the world's best beers come from Mexico; the only way you will ever know is to try them all.

Kahlua: coffee-based liqueur, the national liqueur of Mexico.

Mescal: a very potent, clear liquor much warmer and stronger than tequila, usually served with lime and salt.

Refrecos: soft drinks with mineral water.

Tequila: a strong drink made from the fermented juice of a cactus.

Vino: wine — although Mexico does produce both red and white wines, both sweet and dry, as well as sparkling white wines, they are not well known outside of Mexico.

Tipping. Check to see if your tip has already been included on the bill. If not, a 10 to 20 percent tip is standard.

Unfortunately many tourists experience gastro-intestinal problems before they become accustomed to a new climate, foods, and water (residents of Mexico City may have the same problems when they visit the States). Consult with your physician as to which are the best drugs to prevent or alleviate these digestive ailments. BE SURE TO CARRY THESE PRESCRIPTIONS IN THEIR ORIGINAL CONTAINERS. Water is one of the biggest culprits, and for this reason, many tourists do not drink water unless it is bottled. Unwashed fruit and raw vegetables may also trigger problems. Be aware and be prepared, and you should have no problems.

The value of the dollar and the friendliness of the Mexican people should make your stay in Mexico City for the 1986 World Cup a most pleasant one.

Photo Credits

Appendix
Modern Soccer Training in the U.S.

SOCCER COACHES FROM ALL LEVELS OF PLAY OFTEN WONDER ABOUT HOW TO TRAIN and develop their soccer players so that they will blend into cohesive, attractive, and purposeful teams.

Playing soccer and training to play soccer are closely related to each other. Practices should consist of what the game itself will demand so that players can improve their performance in the next game. Competition is the only true barometer that a coach can use as a guideline for his training sessions.

Every sport has its own cycle, beginning with competitive games and what we learn from these, leading to practice and improvement, and coming back again to competition. Therefore, we can only justify practice sessions that are adjusted to reflect the needs of actual competition. Following this line of thought, we must establish what modern soccer is. Once we have the answer, we can then proceed to find the key to training for modern soccer.

In soccer, as in all other competitive sports, the whole intention is to win. To quote Coach Lombardi, "Winning isn't everything; it's the only thing." However, playing to win by any means (sometimes the wrong means) does not mean that the result is everything. Games should be won in a totally convincing way, where all components of soccer play are brought out. Then the reward is fully satisfying. Ideally, soccer is a combination of a team striving to win coupled with attractive execution of skill and play. The goal of winning is a simple one, while the opinion of how attractively the game is played will vary greatly.

Some believe in functional and purposeful soccer with fast and powerful attacks (eliminating the combination play at midfield), trying to reach the opponent's goal with long passes and finish its attack with shots from any angle. This is typical of the style of play used in the British Isles.

Others believe in a somewhat different approach to attractive play. They only appreciate play carried out by highly skilled individual players. For them, the most important factor is brilliant ball control, bordering on the artistic, with intricate dribblings and surprising tricks. They love individual play and appreciate one-on-one situations. This is the case in the Latin American countries. Comparing the simple and purposeful style of play mentioned earlier, this way of playing soccer gives the impression of a game being played in slow motion. This style can be successful and sometimes is executed with surprising ease. Suddenly, openings appear, and goals are scored.

So there are several schools of thought on how to approach modern training sessions in soccer. The particular style employed is, however, dependent upon the race, national characteristics, mentality, temperment, and imagination of the players. Therefore, different conceptions of ideal soccer will always be formed throughout the world. One great Brazilian soccer player, Marinho, asked one of my staff coaches why the national coach always talks about European soccer and hardly ever mentions Latin-style soccer. The observation was certainly accurate. The reason for this is that the physical and mental make-up of the American soccer player is like that of the European soccer player. We wouldn't expect Steve Pecher or Ricky Davis to be doing sambas with a soccer ball. The environment that they were raised in did not offer samba lessons. This fact must be considered very seriously before we can identify with modern training.

Apart from these different conceptions of what good and attractive soccer is, soccer all over the world has reached a similar stage of development. The defenses are very well organized and have become a higher and more dominant factor than the offense. Even though in theory we tend to say "a good offense is a good defense," in practice it doesn't work. Most coaches are very cautious and depend on a good defense. We must be very concerned about this problem; otherwise all the artistry and beauty of play could die in vain.

So we can say that we have finally identified the problem and/or

recognized the essentials of the modern game. It is characterized by a struggle for superiority between the attack and the defense. For the most part, the defense is winning. A team with real class is one that has the ability to master both parts of the game, being equally effective on the attack and the defense.

To an observer's eyes, a team that can readily achieve this type of play presents itself as a cohesive unit. The obstacles of the game presented to this type of team cannot take them out of their game. Every player on this type of team has a role to play both in defense and in the attack, and everything is methodically planned so that he can be part of an effective whole.

Whether the team is attacking or defending, each player is involved all the time with or without the ball. The overall impression is that the team is defending with all players and attacking with all players. This high level of perfection by a team is demonstrated in a system of play. There are many systems of play and, while there is no need to elaborate here (see my book, *The Official Soccer Book of the United States Soccer Federation*), a general observation is necessary.

What works for one team does not necessarily work for another. The talent and the ability of the individuals is the deciding factor in determining the system of play. The quality of individual players is the priority—not a 4–2–4 or a 3–4–3 formation. As the personalities of the players on the field come and go, so do the systems of play come and go. In the fifties, the Hungarians dominated with a system, but Puskas and Company are gone. In the sixties, it was DiStefano and

Company at Madrid and Charlton and Company in England. They too are gone. In the seventies, it was Pele, and he is gone. Time has run out for Cruyff of Holland as well.

A further consideration of building a class team is the team's ability to master its style. Every player and every team has special abilities and qualities, and these traits require time and practice to mold into an attractive successful unit.

Therefore, the number 1 problem that exists in America today, starting with high-school and college teams, all the way through to pro teams and the National Teams, is lack of preparation time. The American soccer style will never develop unless the players and coaches are given the opportunity to develop their qualities in a modern, year-round, playing-and-training environment. Until a system that will allow for this is developed, we will always play below the standards we are trying to achieve.

We can easily say that when a team is confident of itself and has reached its fullest means, it can go out on the field and play its own game. We can then say that this team has truly arrived with real class. This has not been the case in America by any team to date.

It is important to remember that there are teams that can play excellent soccer as closely knit units yet can never be among the highest class of teams. This is typical of amateur and pro teams in America. The reason for this is that they can only play at certain speeds. If the speed of the game increases beyond that level, they lose their confidence, assertiveness, and attractiveness of play. They cannot perform at optimal speeds where there is

little time and space to execute their skills or tactics. This has been proven year in and year out as our pro clubs and National Teams travel to Europe and find it difficult to play and perform successfully. A well-played team therefore is not a team of real class. The real class team is one that can perform at top speed.

Do not confuse playing at high speed with running at high speed. It's how fast you can play—not how fast you can run. This is the difference between the modern game today and the game as it was played years ago. The modern player plans his options to play the ball before it arrives at his feet, not after. When I played, I was taught the principle of "trap, look, then pass." Today, with this approach, a soccer player would be lost.

We can say then that the modern game is one that requires a team to perform and solve the problems of defense and attack in concert with utilizing a playing system that complements the qualities of its players, who can express their skill and knowledge at top speed for the entire game.

The modern training program should revolve around the knowledge of the principles on which the game of soccer is built. Recognizing the demands the modern game puts on our players sets the stage for the aims and objectives of our training programs. The most important aim of a coach is to build teamwork. This means each individual player is molded in such a way that the team is a cohesive unit. Each player must learn and understand his role in attack and defense. The age of one-way players has passed us. The player's ability to play without the ball (move into open space) and his ability to mark a man are now the priorities. However, this means that each player must perform at higher skill levels than ever before, since the opponent will also now provide tight marking and quick movement of the ball.

We can now establish some ground rules in our training sessions regarding how we can go about preparing and training our players. The aims would be:

1. to make sure we have gained optimal performance from each individual player;
2. to mold the individual player into a solid unit that possesses skill and the will to win (toughness); and
3. to make sure that each player physically has reached his potential of speed, strength, power, and endurance that will enable him to play the full game at the same pace.

The aims of training are very clear. They are derived from the game itself. the strength and foundation of any well-played game relies on fitness, technique, and tactics, along with mental toughness. These components are inseparable. They belong together and should be addressed at all training sessions. It is very possible to employ the same training exercises to better fitness levels, skill levels, and tactical play.

The approach is methodical with an introduction to an exercise, to a fundamental stage of learning, and then on to a match-related stage where an opponent is introduced. The opponent provides passive play and then actual play, forcing the player with the ball to be aware of the opponent's presence.

The learning process here is that the player coordinates his movement of the body to the ball without pressure and expresses his technique and then, finally, under pressure, transfers the technique into applied skill in match-like conditions. This develops the player's own personal rhythm and, to a degree, fitness.

But ball control and tactics cannot be expressed without properly fit players. Ball control and tactical knowledge without fitness is like an engine without fuel. The team that is best fit, assuming it has the other components, will more often than not win the game.

Small-sided games developed for team practice are a very important part of a training program. They are parts taken from a full-sided game. If presented under match-like conditions, they are considered among the best means of training and improving the player's technical, tactical, and physical requirements for the game.

These exercises are enjoyable to a player, and he immediately begins to identify and relate the exercises to the game in which he will play. The small-sided games are performed in a progressional manner, beginning with 1 v. 1.

This exercise teaches immediately the competitive spirit of trying to win the ball from the opponent or maintain possession of the ball. These are very important factors in the modern game. Other benefits derived from this exercise include alertness, concentration, quick reaction, and fast feet. This exercise helps determine how players will behave in individual duals under match conditions with an adversary. Fighting for possession of the ball is a battle of wits and knowledge of the game on a smaller scope. Body swerves, feints, tricks, and dribbling are all expressed in this exercise. Another benefit of 1 v. 1 exercises is that they are a good lesson in quick adaptability when the situation changes from attack to defense and vice versa.

In the end result, two things we aim to achieve from the 1 v. 1 exercise are:

1. to give the player a thorough practice in winning the ball; and
2. to introduce two small goals in a confined space and have the players go to goal. The ultimate purpose in any soccer practice is to finish on goal. The attraction of scoring goals should serve as a reminder that winning the ball is only step A and going to goal and scoring is step B—and the end result.

Ideally, a coach would like to develop tactics in which his team has numerical superiority over the opponent. Obviously, this superiority must be formed in the area the ball is, for there is where the danger lies.

Possession time of the ball usually determines the winner. Therefore, the next progression would be to form pairs or groups around the ball. The greater the number of players or contact pairs around the ball, the more options the player with the ball has. The more options players have, the greater the chances they have for superiority over the opponent and the better the possibility of winning the game. We like

to strive to have an ideal of two options for the player in possession of the ball to play or pass to. More often than not, having an overabundance of options creates problems for the player with the ball, as he now must make the most positive decision. Very often cases of overchoice, the player with the ball chooses the least positive option.

We begin by introducing exercises that are the foundation in forming concepts about team play and performance. Two against one is played in a confined space, with the one player taking on a destructive role and the two players attempting to move the ball into open space, forming angles and interpassing the ball. In this exercise, a good pair begins to develop surprise moves on the opponent and begins to read each other's movements. Understanding and reading each other's movements is one of the most difficult tasks to achieve in developing teamwork. The principle role in a 2 v. 1 exercise is controlled by the man with the ball. He must decide whether to play the ball one-touch, to hold the ball when it is necessary, or to play the ball accurately to feet or space, with the proper pace on the ball, using bending or straight passes.

By dribbling the ball and twisting or turning his body, a player can create new angles for a pass to his teammate. Understanding each other in feints and deceptions against an opponent makes for an attractive and well-played pair of players.

The player who is defending against the two has his tactical role as well. He cannot blindly dive into tackles. He must try to outwit the two, by making them think that they have deceived him by their play. He then quickly makes an attempt to win the ball.

Making space and creating openings for penetrating passes is accomplished by interpassing movements. Three against one is an exercise that can make all this a happening. The most important consideration in a 3 v. 1 exercise is that one player always supports the man in possession. This immediately creates openings. Fast direct play on the part of the three will have the one defender going crazy, with no chance of intercepting the ball. The 3 v. 1 exercise is obviously a situation in superiority of numbers of players against the one.

The freedom of movement of the ball with sharp, one-touch interpassing tires and discourages the opponent, keeping him from thinking of his own attack. For the defender, the situation remains hopeless so long as the three move fast with the player in possession of the ball executing accurate passes and the two teammates running in deceptive patterns. The benefits are reaped when all three players play with composure

and use their soccer intellect to break down the opponent.

To take the 3 v. 1 exercise to its fullest, we introduce a match-related tactical play situation, placing a winger on the left side of the field at midfield with another front runner near him, and a supporting halfback behind the two. The defender would be a fullback who is positioned on the right side of the field. From here, the three attack the goal with different movements. For example, one option would be for the halfback to make a pass to his wing. At the same time, the other attacker makes a sprint toward the touchline. The winger then makes a penetrating pass and continues to run in the direction of the goal, but in the position of the other attacker. The halfback supports the play downfield.

Several other variations can be added in this exercise. Finally, the exercise should be performed under match-like conditions in which the attacking players make their own decisions as to how to go to goal successfully and finish.

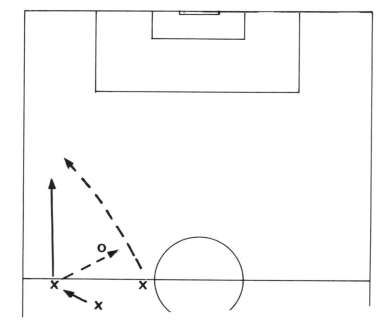

Moving from the 3 v.1, we set up exercises for 3 v. 2 with an approach similar to that of 3 v. 1. The two defenders could well be a fullback and a wingback. The attacking players are exposed to different purposeful movements against two defenders under passive defensive play. The attacking players, playing under match-like conditions, attempt to finish on goal.

The aim of these exercises is to reach a level of training where a square pass is followed by a through pass, and where successful dribbling is followed by an accurate pass or by a solo run finished off by a shot on goal. In all our small-sided games, we should be teaching our defenders how to defend against superior numbers.

As a coach, you should continue to introduce players to other tactical exercises such as 4 v. 2, 4 v. 3, 4 v. 4, and 5 v. 4. All these exercises can be taught in the same progressional way as we demonstrated in doing 1 v. 1, 2 v. 1, 3 v. 1 and 3 v. 2. Placing restrictions such as one-touch, two touches, dribble before passing, sprint after passing, etc., help quicken the learning process during tactical exercises.

The last stage of team tactical development is team tactics. Here we begin to introduce units of exercise which would include 6 v. 4 half-field to goal, 8 v. 8 full-field, or 11 v.11 full-field. In these exercises, the focal point is the concentration of mid-field play.

Regardless of what playing system is being used, the midfielders thread the play by running together. The midfielders take on both attacking and defending roles. The general aim of the midfielders is to draw the opposition's defense from its goal and into the midfield area. They try to keep the defense on the move by frequently changing direction from side to side in an attempt to force the defense to regroup itself and to create gaps for quick penetrating passes. The faster the midfield play is executed, the faster the opponent is found in a confused, disorganized state.

The central figures of midfield play in the fifties and sixties were usually the two halfbacks and two inside forwards. There were exceptions to the rule. Some countries would withdraw their center forward such as Didi for Brazil and DeStefano of Real Madrid in Spain. However, for the most part, we would like to think that we are dealing with a minimum of three midfielders and a maximum of four.

So we begin to develop exercises of 4 v. 2 with the intention of making square passes in an attempt to split the two defenders, making a penetrating pass possible. Slowly, we begin to introduce other parts to the machine. The wings are added, and play at midfield is finally turned over to the winger, from which point the attack begins. The center forward is left out on purpose so that all the buildup at midfield is directed to the wing. After some time, the center forward is introduced to the scheme of midfield, and again different square passes are executed by the midfield until a gap is opened and the center forward becomes a target for a pass. This team tactic plan is completed with a shot on goal.

This is just one of many examples of how we can go about developing a cohesive unit on a soccer field—one that has total understanding of each player's individual movements. To build a successful cohesive unit requires time, knowledge, and understanding of how to go about preparing an engine that will work on all cylinders. Indeed, I found it very difficult to build a strong national team made up of all-star players, with only one or two weeks of training/preparation time.

The modern methods of coaching soccer players require that all sessions include fitness, technique, and tactics, from which a player also derives mental toughness. It is very important that a coach has a very good understanding of what the needs are for his team in the order of priority. Many incompetents have worked in the game in America, and possibly they have become a major obstacle in our growth as a quality soccer country.

As we strive for perfection in execution, more often than not we will see that many problems are created by the poor technical and/or tactical performance of the individual players in a team concept. This simply leads the coach to identify the individual problems of each of his players and correct them with functional training or individualized training. Here we begin to identify the problem as being of a technical nature or a tactical nature (assuming that fitness is not a problem).

Functional *technical* training would be used in cases where a player has difficulty, for example, heading a ball under pressure. An exercise for this purpose would be organized to correct this problem. It could be repetitive heading with an opponent providing pressure. Possibly, it could be that the problem lies with the player's vertical jump, which would mean improving his strength and power. By looking into the

player's problem in depth, the coach can bring out and correct his weaknesses so that he can become a more solid performer in the machine.

The functional *tactical* problem of a player is often more difficult to recognize than a player's technical or physical problem. In this sense, the coach is dealing with the player's mind and his ability to get involved in the game. The problems may be due to lack of timing, concentration, anticipation, perception, and/or reading the game. The use of video aids such as game films or tapes helps to identify the tactical problem of an individual. Once the coach has pinpointed the player's tactical weakness, he can create exercises to improve the player's performance. For example, it is possible that one of the front runners has difficulty in running to the near post when the ball is on the baseline and being served to that position. It may be that the player overruns the serve or gets to the near post too late. The coach then creates this situation in practice and has the player read the serve and time his run. This form of specialized training in the tactical sense will again help the player to reach his potential as an individual and in turn will help him to be more effective in team play and tactical execution.

The final stage of recognizing problems is the ability of players to execute the technical-tactical skills in a team concept. The work here is to improve the individual's technical-tactical skills, which the player would then incorporate into the total picture for effective team play. It is very important that a coach has the expertise and knowledge to study and understand the player's technical-tactical skill weaknesses so that he can correct them with effective exercise in a team concept.

First and foremost, the problems may be in the player's physical fitness qualities which may be having an effect on his technical-tactical skills. To recognize this problem, as an example, the coach might check the player's speed. It may be that the player does a

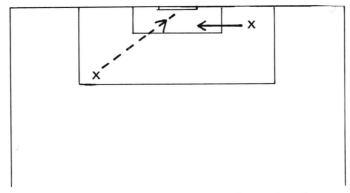

40-yard sprint in 5.5 seconds, while the norm is 4.8. Even though he has good technical and tactical skills, his speed is not that of the team norm. This, consequently, may take him out of team play. He may be getting to the ball too late, etc. The coach then needs to work with the player to improve his speed over that distance provided that the player genetically has the speed qualities necesary to reach the team norm.

To assess a player's technical-tactical skills, the following methods should be used:

1. evaluation by a coach (playing experience is needed, but not necessarily of international class);
2. visual aids, tape machines, etc.
3. statistics taken during game for

individual players (faulty passes, faulty receptions, etc.)

After gathering the information on the players from the above criteria, the coach should then consider the following points:

1. the system in which player plays, as well as his role in the system;
2. the player's fitness level, both physical and mental, and;
3. balance of training between players as a team and as individuals.

To improve the individual's technical skills on the highest level of play (assuming that he has mastered the skills in a relatively low-paced game), we increase his intensity in work to a point where his heart is working at 160–80 heartbeats per minute. He now must master the ball while running at full speed. The highest form of technical execution is when a player can perform and exhibit his skill when he is running at optimal speed.

To improve both the technical and the tactical skills, we play 7 v. 6 to half-field with a goalkeeper. We would allow the winger to reach the baseline and serve the ball to the near post. While the right winger is going to the baseline to receive a pass, an opposite front runner makes a run for the near post. In this exercise, the technical-tactical skill is practiced both by the server from the baseline and the near-post runner. Timing and reading on the part of both players is one of the priorities (tactical), while the serve and the finishing is the other (technical).

While attempting to improve the technical-tactical skills, it is essential to encourage players to concentrate and communicate with their eyes to relate the exercises more closely to match-like conditions. At all times, it should be stressed that it is the responsibility of the players to make the tactical decisions that will result in a possible score—if the technical execution is performed at top class.

In summary, a coach must have a very good understanding of what is needed in his training programs for his players in the technical, tactical, and physical consideration if his team is to have success. Knowing his players

through keen observation during game conditions will help him modify his training program according to the needs of his players. Taking exercises at random to fill time during training programs would be criminal. One solid training session consisting of one and one-half hours is more than sufficient to obtain full benefits.

If training begins with a preseason program and the team has two scheduled practices per day, the morning session should normally be of a technical nature and the late afternoon or evening session should be of a tactical and physical nature. The nervous system is fully at rest in the morning. Therefore, the skill execution is more concentrated and more positive benefits result. Less running with strength and power and more relaxed movement to execute the skill early in the season is sufficient. In the evening and after regeneration, the body gains more energy and is willing to work harder off the ball in tactical small-sided games or 11 v. 11.

Finally, we must make it very clear

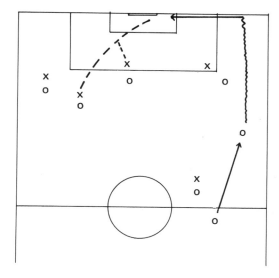

that the modern methods of coaching can be applied to all levels of play. The genius of each coach is to prescribe for his players what is necessary for them. He is the only person who knows his own players' capabilities.

Modern American Youth Training

In observing the tremendous growth of soccer in our country, one begins to wonder what methods can be implemented in our soccer coaching so we have "instant" success in the development of our soccer players. We have heard, in the past thirty years or so, all kinds of recommendations and suggestions from domestic and foreign experts as to how to find this instant success.

I have attended numerous clinics and conventions since the late fifties, and it was constantly told us by foreign experts how we should solve our problems. In ten years, they said, the U.S. would become a world power. Well, we are now in the 1980s, and we are still striving to become a world power in soccer. The various suggestions and recommendations of coaches from abroad were to some degree useful, and we have learned from them. However, one wonders how coaches from abroad had so much insight into our problems without ever being involved in U.S. soccer or even kicking a soccer ball on U.S. soil.

Whatever has transpired in the last eighty years in U.S. soccer development, we can honestly say that the quality of coaches and players began to grow in the late sixties. Of course, many of our older fellow coaches will not agree. In 1969, with the formation

of the national coaching schools, things started to happen.

Dettmar Cramer's arrival on the U.S. soccer scene helped considerably. His convincing ability immediately impressed the country, and his knowledge of the immediate needs for the country started soccer on the right course. Emphasis was placed on technique and economical coaching methods to improve technique.

There was very little difficulty in convincing coaches of these priorities since it came from Dettmar, considered to be the one responsible for developing soccer successfully in Japan. He is also a master in technique, and his demonstrations never left anyone in doubt. So, for the past dozen years, we have witnessed a tremendous growth in technical development.

The next major concern is to combine the technique learning with movement. By this, we mean having players execute all ball skills while in full motion or running almost at full speed. This type of training is the immediate need of our players. Having total command of the ball while running at top speed is what most of your quality foreign players are capable of executing.

The other problem is to convince our coaches to prepare their athletes to become total soccer players and not positional players. If we can expose our players to every skill that belongs to soccer and have these players execute these skills in the three parts of the field, then we will be able to recognize complete soccer players rather than seeing only positional players. Once our players have learned to play the game, we can help them in finding a position on the field where they feel most comfortable in relation to their teammates. To this day, most coaches will assign a position for a player and then work with him. This approach slows his growth in soccer as a player, and slows the growth of soccer in the U.S. We can use an example of another sport's development—basketball. I'm not so sure basketball has developed a coaching school and a method to improve basketball players. What has happened is that players learned on their own by playing "schoolyard basketball." Then coaches take the already skilled player and put him into a position. We also, in soccer, need "backyard soccer" to improve skill and develop a complete game for players. Then, soccer coaches can place the players in positions. Coaches should eliminate positions in the early stages of a player's development, playing small-sided games so that players learn to attack and defend equally as well.

The training of young players requires more small-sided games with small fields and small goals. Ideal field size would be similar to that of the indoor soccer facilities used in the U.S. Seven-a-side plus a goalkeeper would be the competitive league requirement. However, in actual training, playing 3 v. 3 to one or two goals is an excellent way of allowing the young players to grow both physically and mentally. If there is one area where the American coaches overdo it, it's overcoaching. Some of the greatest players in the world have learned to play on the beaches of Brazil, backyards of Germany, and streets of Argentina. The American coach must encourage this type of training for our youth as well.